MANDALA

Distributed in the Commonwealth and Europe
by Routledge & Kegan Paul Ltd
London and Henley-on-Thames

MANDALA

José and Miriam Argüelles

Foreword by Chögyam Trungpa

SHAMBALA: Berkeley and London

1972

SHAMBALA PUBLICATIONS, INC.
1409 Fifth Street
Berkeley, California 94710
and
Barn Cottage, Stert
Devizes, Wiltshire, England

© copyright by José and Miriam Argüelles
and Shambala Publications, Inc.
ISBN 0-87773-033-4
LCC 70-189856
Book Design by Hal Hershey

Front cover: *Mandala of Yamantaka.* Tibetan Tanka.
Courtesy of the Center of Asian Art and Culture.
The Avery Brundage Collection; San Francisco, California.
Back cover: *Mandala of Nuclear Light.* Miriam Argüelles.

Color separations by Solzer & Hail, San Francisco, California.
Printing and binding by Bradford Printing, Denver, Colorado.

The Godrooted heart blooms in wonderway.

Contents

Foreword *by Chögyam Trungpa* / 8

Preface / 9

Man Must Remake Himself Within the Eternity of His Own Body
I. The Universality of the Mandala / 11

I Am the Mandala of the Light Eye Give
II. The Mandala as a Visual Process / 23

According to the Sacred and Magical Art: I Am That
III. The Mandala as Art Form / 33

So That In Me the Plan Illumined Grows
IV. The Mandala as a Key to Symbolic Systems / 53

To Become One as the Flower Wedded to the Sun
V. The Ritual of the Mandala / 81

And Through the Sun Beyond What Even Man or Flower Knows
VI. The Mandala as a Point of Departure / 107

Bibliography / 130

Foreword

The search for knowledge and wisdom by concepts is part of man's confused struggle. Nevertheless using ideas as a stepping stone is necessary for the student as a starting point.

Mandala in the broad sense is all-encompassing space which accommodates the self-existing cosmic structure, radiating different energies: pacifying, magnetizing, increasing, destroying.

In this book the authors have worked diligently, delving into many different cultures and studying the expressions of Buddha nature in each tradition, particularly in terms of the Mandala principle. As such, their work is itself a demonstration of Mandala in action.

The paths that the reason will follow going through this book may bring confusion as well as affirmation, but this experience can also be regarded as an expression of Mandala in action because both positive and negative experiences are part of the contents of the Mandala. The awakening of the underlying intelligence is the only starting point.

It is my hope that this book will give you new insight in transcending the world of psychological and spiritual materialism.

Chögyam Trungpa, Rinpoche
Karma Dzong
Boulder, Colorado

February 25, 1972

Preface

It was in the spring of 1967 that we began painting Mandalas together. As our work developed, interest grew both in the finished products as well as in the process by which the paintings were executed. From our own reflections, and in response to an increasing demand, we began to offer seminars and workshops in an effort at guiding others toward an understanding and working capacity for applying the Mandala to their own lives. Flowing naturally from these various endeavors was this book which we undertook some two years ago. Writing and production has been another slowly and patiently developed Mandala. Often we were confronted by mute images awaiting the formative call of the word, and there were no words available. Through contemplation and love were the words retrieved, the images formed. At times our researches took us far afield, but there was always return. It is our hope that these efforts will furnish an appropriate introduction to a topic that is essentially inexhaustible.

José and Miriam Argüelles

Man Must Remake Himself Within the Eternity of His Own Body

The Universality of the Mandala

The Vegetative Universe opens like a flower
from the earth's center
in which is Eternity...

William Blake

The earth is a living Mandala—a structural matrix through and from which flow a succession of changes, elemental forms, and primal surges, each surpassing the other in an infinite variety of organic structures and impulses, crowned by the supreme attribute of reflective consciousness. Its flow, though working through a relatively well-defined structure, is subject to the infinite processes of growth and transformation by virtue of the ever-changing relationships both internal and external to its basic structure.

A Mandala consists of a series of concentric forms, suggestive of a passage between different dimensions. In its essence, it pertains not only to the earth but to the macrocosm and microcosm, the largest structural processes as well as the smallest. It is the gatepost between the two.

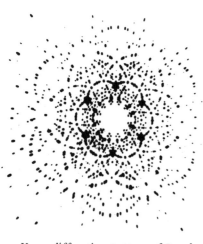

X-ray diffraction pattern of Beryl.

The wise man looks into space and does not regard the small as too little nor the great as too big; for he knows that there is no limit to dimensions.

Lao Tzu

Whirlpool Galaxy in Canes Venatici.

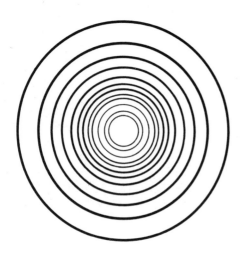

The Mandala is earth and man, both the atom that composes the material essence of man, and the galaxy of which the earth is but an atom. Through the concept and structure of the Mandala man may be projected into the universe and the universe into man. Such mutual interpenetration is the synthesis of the various polarizing tendencies now manifest upon the planet.

The universality of the Mandala is in its one constant, *the principle of the center.* The center is the beginning of the Mandala as it is the beginning and origin of all form and of all processes, including the extensions of form into time. *In the Beginning was the Center:* the center of the mind of God, the eternal Creator, the Dream of Brahman, the galaxies that swirl beyond the lenses of our great telescopes. In all of these the center is one, and in the center lies eternity.

The center is symbolic of the eternal potential. From the same inexhaustible source all seeds grow and develop, all cells realize their function; even down to the atom there is none without its nucleus, its sun-seed about which revolve its component particles. As in the atom, so in the stars—modern thought only confirms the ancient Hermetic adage, "As above, so below."

There is a structural law, a cosmic principle by which perceptible forms are sustained, and which governs the processes of transformation in all things. This can be realized only because the center principle manifests itself through man in the same ways as it does through a flower or a star; in it we may discover our cosmic commonality—our cosmic community.

The center of the Mandala is not only the external constant of space but also of time. The center of time is *now.* It is the burning tip of awareness, undefinable, for any definition in time exhausts what is *now,* and yet there is nothing but *now* and *now* is all that will ever exist. Though we can speak of past and future, the *symmetry* aspects of *now,* these only exist by virtue of the undefinable and eternal. This eternal *now* and the realization of one's center are coeval, simultaneous events. Living totally *now,* one's existence unfolds like a Mandala. At the core, each man is the center of his own compass and experiences, his own *cardinal points*—North, South, East, and West.

We are defined not only by our place on the physical level, but by our position in consciousness, and these are an interdependent whole. *Now* is the focalization of a continuum, interrupted only by forgetfulness. The center exists continually, first as a seed, then as a stem, the trunk or the spine, and finally in the flower, where a new seed is produced. In man, consciousness—the energy and source-seed of his evolutive future—manifests through all his *nows* as so many Mandalas, so many centers around which are grouped the constituent elements of awareness. Like ripples in a pond, each awareness-moment expands out from its own center, containing in its form-pattern the configuration of all phenomena in the universe, material and immaterial. And so the process of centering—the gathering of oneself as if by an inward throw of a stone into the pool of one's own consciousness—is also a Mandala.

Universally inherent in man's consciousness, the Mandala has continually appeared in his constructions, rituals and art forms. From its various manifestations we can derive three basic properties:

a center
symmetry
cardinal points

The first principle is constant; the latter two vary according to the nature of the particular Mandala. Symmetry can be bilateral or dynamic—rigid and well-defined, or absolutely fluid. The cardinal points may be precise in number, the amount depending upon the Mandala situation; or the points may be infinite, and nonexistent as in a circle.

In Sanskrit Mandala literally means circle and center. Its traditional design often utilizes the circle—symbol of the cosmos in its entirety—and the square—symbol of the earth or of the man-made world. In the *I Ching,* one of the most ancient of texts, this symbolism corresponds to *yang*—the male, originating, celestial principle—and *yin*—the female, receptive, earth principle.

In Tibet the Mandala has achieved its fullest and most complex development—both as an artistic form and as a meditative ritual emphasizing cosmic integration. The center, the abode of the deity, is contained within the square—the palace of inner being—surrounded by a circle or series of circles, each symbolizing a particular phase of initiation or level of consciousness.

To Westerners, the popular reintroduction of the Mandala concept can be specifically traced to the work of Carl G. Jung, who rediscovered the Mandala as a basic structural device in the alchemical tradition of the West, and as a therapeutic, integrative art form created by patients in their own search for individuation. In *The Secret of the Golden Flower,* Jung and the Orientalist Richard C. Wilhelm relate the idea of the Mandala as a therapeutic device to the Mandala as a ritual, meditative technique conducive to mystic exaltation. In either, the aim is a higher level of integration, though in the Eastern tradition

Snow crystal.

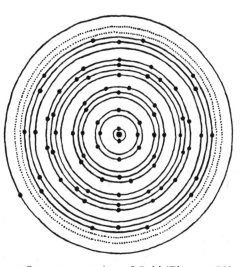

A flat representation of Gold (Element 79).

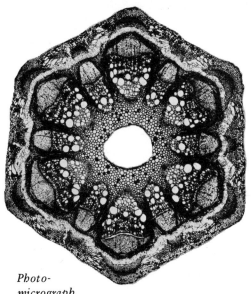

Photo-micrograph of a cross section of a twig.

Mandala of Kalachakra.

the Mandala is essentially a vehicle for concentrating the mind so that it may pass beyond its usual fetters. In its own way, the Mandala as a therapeutic tool achieves the same end, for in projecting his own mental complexes upon the cosmic grid of the Mandala, the patient exorcises his mind, and liberates himself from his various mental obsessions. For this very reason the Mandala must be constructed with great care and concentration. It symbolizes various levels of awareness within the individual as well as the energy that unifies and heals. Making a Mandala is a universal *activity*, a self-integrating ritual.

The process of the Navaho sandpainting offers many parallels to the Tibetan Mandala ritual and *yantra:* all are by nature a complete meditation, with the mind in right perspective so that it can't escape anywhere. The formal similarity between the Tibetan and Southwest Indian Mandalas reveals healing—the curing of psychosomatic symptoms—as an integral aspect of meditation. The basic structure of the sandpainting exemplifies the universal characteristics of the Mandala: its center is the center of the cosmos, the place where the person being healed may sit. Symmetrically placed about the center are the cardinal points, often symbolizing the directions, elements and seasons. Condensed in this simple form of a sandpainting is the interdependence of all phenomena and their essential unity in time by virtue of their relationship with the one eternal center.

The healing, meditative, integrative purpose of the Mandala has its beginning and its root in man's attempt at self-orientation. Man is the center of his own relative time/space locus from which he receives a cosmic consecration. Whatever is in front, behind, to the left, and right of him become the four cardinal directions; whatever is above and below become the heavens and the earth; what was yesterday and will be tomorrow becomes time past and time future—and the center is always the individual, the bearer of the awareness of the eternal *now*.

Feeling the impulse toward wholeness, man applies it to all that he does. It motivates his thoughts, permeates his activities, and resides in all that he constructs. In his dwellings, as in those of most of the "primitive," pre-industrial world, there is a place, an altar, a fire, a stone that is the center, not only of the house or dwelling, but also of the entire cosmos. This is no inherent contradiction, for we are dealing with what is essentially a *sacred* principle, or a sacred state of consciousness in which all beings and all things are realized equally as emanations of One Divine Whole. Sacred consciousness, of which the Mandala is a structural model, conforms to the Hermetic statement, "God is an intelligent sphere whose center is everywhere and whose circumference is nowhere."

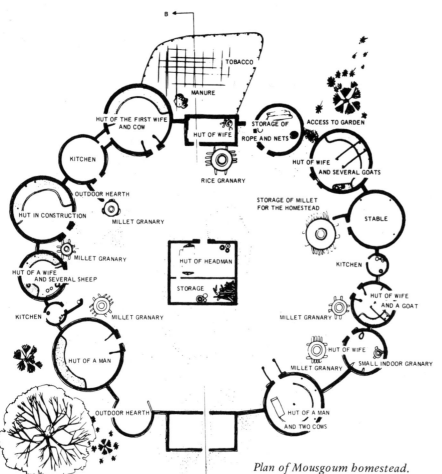

Plan of Mousgoum homestead.
Gaia, Cameroun, Africa.

In our present culture we are far from the situation of those people for whom everything is sacred—for whom the tribe is a sacred social unit and the tribal structure itself a reflection of the divine whole, an imprint of the heavens, stamped upon every act, every artifact and dwelling. While we no longer share the same communal, mandaloid consciousness of our ancestors or those still able to maintain a traditional way of life, individually we may still bring ourselves to the same, primal existential condition. No matter how civilized we become, we must still answer for ourselves the basic question of self-orientation, and in this respect, our condition today is no different than that of our first ancestors stepping out of the forest into the light. In this situation the inherent healing power of the Mandala begins to reassert itself.

A properly drawn mandala is a book in itself containing a great deal of information but he who would read the symbols must learn the language.

Robert S. De Ropp

The Center and the Polarities

Though the principle of the center is One, the patterns, the swirls and eddies of form and process which are generated by and through the center are infinite; and though infinite in number, the centers are essentially one, for each is the same irreducible point, the primary syllable, the word, the Logos, through which all is uttered and through which all must pass. This is the significance of the mystic syllable OM, which in its way is the seed center of all sound as the point is of vision. For ourselves there are two movements which can be defined by any number of directions: a movement toward and a movement away; a forward movement, the movement of birth, is away from the center point toward the world of differentiation; a backward movement toward the point is the movement of death, or reabsorption in the realm of infinite potential. These two movements and their poles, birth and death, define the basic polarities which circumscribe existence as we now know it. Actually, the polarities are but the two extremes perceptible to us of one and the same motion.

The basic attribute by which our consciousness is defined is that of *contrast*. As in the well-known *t'ai chi* symbol, the paradigm of the nature of our consciousness, the two basic elements—*yin* and *yang*—exist by virtue of simultaneous contrast; only together do they exist and only together do they form a whole, symbolized by the circle circumscribing them. We live immersed in an ocean of polarities: life and death, man and woman, weak and strong, high and low, happy and sad, black and white. In the most incredible ways, not only our consciousness, but our language as well as contemporary social structures and techniques are based upon and permeated with the ramifications of the primal polarities. Our error is to think of these as absolutes, however defined. This issues from a limitation in our conscious experience, at least as it has so far been developed and structured. The way consciousness is normally oriented today, only the polarities are witnessed and experienced, so that, without the knowledge of their common ground—the center point—all that is experienced is the constant struggle, the battles and wars waged against self-created and self-perpetuated antagonists. Without a grounding in the center, it can be said of man that if he had no enemy he would find it necessary to invent one!

The *center* and the *polarities:* these are the keys that unlock the language of the Mandala, as it is the Mandala that can burst the fetters of man's internal bondage and conflict by leading him to a viewpoint from which the various polarities may be harmonized. All understanding, knowledge, and principles, based as they are upon the primal duality of earthly consciousness, bow before the mystery of the center, the point from which all goes forth and to which all returns. The polarities of birth and death, the attraction and repulsion of forms and forces, the past and the future are held together by the instantaneous yet eternal seed-center—the mysterious present. And these polarities: what are they but mirror-phases of the varieties of growth and transformation transmitted from the seed-centers, the points through which energy is dispersed or focalized, transformed or reborn?

Centering, healing and *growth* define the rhythms of the Mandala process. By concentrating its energy an organism is able to heal itself, grow, and expand beyond itself. Healing and growth have meaning only as responses to those crises which every organism encounters. These crises are a "normal," integral aspect of the living process, defining the junctures of growth, much as the joints of a bamboo define the length of a stalk. However, it is the individual's responses to crises that determine whether he continues developing in the direc-direction of the light or the darkness, toward a new, enlarged capacity for being, or toward a condition of stasis and decay.

From the point of view of the Mandala, there are no "good" or "bad" aspects to situations, much less good or bad experiences: all experiences are equal in the sense that they happen at all. It is the individual's task not to assign ethical definitions to his experiences but to accept them equally, to as-similate them and understand the lesson they hold for him. The Mandala as a construct enables the individual to better accept his experiences, for it provides a general plan or scheme upon which they may be projected and plotted out in relationship to their opposites or antitheses. In this way the totality of any situation is understood and integrated; a union of opposites has been achieved, and another stage of growth has been initiated.

The Mandala is a basic tool for the second major phase of growth which human beings undergo—that which begins where the essentials of physical growth leave off (though certainly the physical transformation processes do not cease until the point of death.) Up to the time of physical maturation basic attention is paid to the physical coordination of the organism. After the peak of maturation and the physical limits have been tested, the focus of attention slowly shifts inward to the development and coordination of more intuitive capacities.

As a tool in this process of growth, the mutual interaction of the compon-ent parts of the Mandala aids the individual concentrating upon it by increasing his own sense of self-relatedness. Every part is related and gives support to every other part; in nature this is easily seen in the snowflake or in a microsco-pic sea creature. Each is an organic whole, an utter economy of form and energy allowing the entity to achieve its function with maximum ease.

As with these minute organisms, so with man. However, by the intricacy of his development and the resulting malleability of his structure, man exhibits a greater capacity for structural integration and transformative possibilities. By their complex nature human energies tend to diffuse and scatter, impeding the

Photomicrograph of the Arachnoidisus Ehrenbergii.

tremendous potential for growth. Essentially, each human being is a Mandala unto himself; but this Mandala must be developed and created anew for each individual. Each man must concentrate himself, realize his own polar coordinates and reach his center in order to unlock the energies contained within. Put in another way, every Mandala, every organism is a whole; as Dane Rudhyar has suggested, each organism is a focalization of the entire universe at one given space/time interval, and likewise, each space/time interval is such a focalization.

Among the Tibetans the Mandala places the meditator in complete identification with its existing pattern. The meditator experiences his essential relatedness to the cosmic rhythms. This renewed sense of relatedness is the self-revelation of an organic whole. The meditator intuits that not only is he a set of on-going interrelationships of structures and systems, but that this set can only exist within a greater frame of reference.

Finite and infinite—the very concept is but one of the constructs which the Mandala is intended to lead us beyond. The Mandala is a module exhibiting principles of organicity: interrelationship of parts, interdependence of systems, resonance and synchronicity.

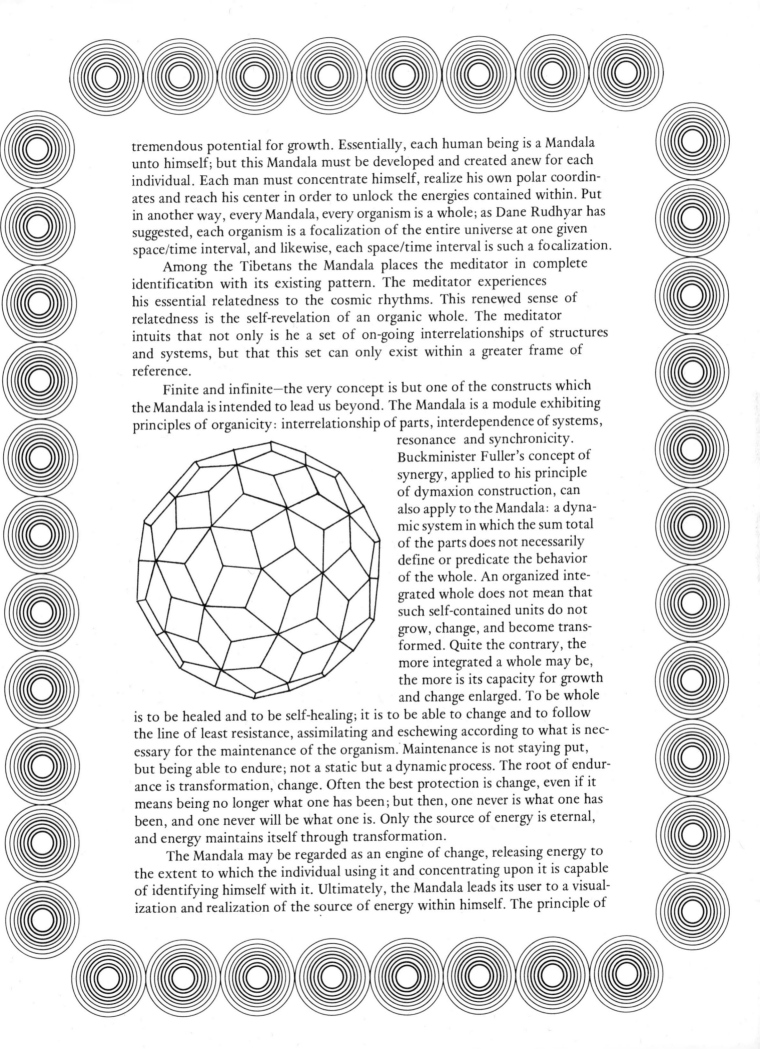

Buckminister Fuller's concept of synergy, applied to his principle of dymaxion construction, can also apply to the Mandala: a dynamic system in which the sum total of the parts does not necessarily define or predicate the behavior of the whole. An organized integrated whole does not mean that such self-contained units do not grow, change, and become transformed. Quite the contrary, the more integrated a whole may be, the more is its capacity for growth and change enlarged. To be whole is to be healed and to be self-healing; it is to be able to change and to follow the line of least resistance, assimilating and eschewing according to what is necessary for the maintenance of the organism. Maintenance is not staying put, but being able to endure; not a static but a dynamic process. The root of endurance is transformation, change. Often the best protection is change, even if it means being no longer what one has been; but then, one never is what one has been, and one never will be what one is. Only the source of energy is eternal, and energy maintains itself through transformation.

The Mandala may be regarded as an engine of change, releasing energy to the extent to which the individual using it and concentrating upon it is capable of identifying himself with it. Ultimately, the Mandala leads its user to a visualization and realization of the source of energy within himself. The principle of

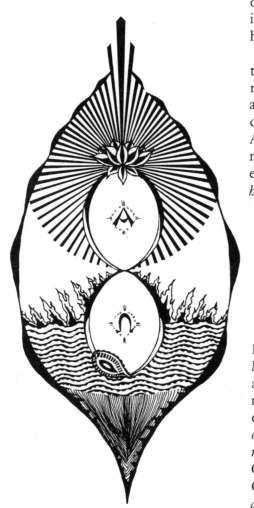

the Mandala lies not in the external form, which is unique for each situation, but in the center, the source through which the form-creating energy flows. To be integrated, to be made whole, means to be able to maintain contact with one's center. Mandala is a *centering* technique, a process of consciously following a path to one's center. A fully individuated being, no matter what may occur to him outwardly, is able to maintain contact with this center, to assimilate and recreate all experience without losing touch with the vital source of his very being.

In a world that is split, divided by the "Civil War of Man," healing is needed to make whole. Mandala is a whole-ing technique; it is the alchemy of opposites reuniting, a blueprint that can be placed upon anything, or any man or being. It is a vision, it is a song, it is a story and a dance—the infinitely renewed seed that contains in its nucleus the collective dream of its kind, the energy of its species. And so with man, who is but the seed of Divine Energy, the plant of which is mankind mandalized. Mandala is a technique for the creation of this vital energy within the individual. *Man must remake himself within the eternity of his own body.*

Notes

Literature concerning the Mandala is not extensive. Most of it deals with the Mandala as a sacred art form of the Orient, and although some thinkers—such as Eliade and Jung—have related the Mandala to other cultures and traditions, no one has developed a concept of its universality to any extent. Basic references for the Oriental traditions include: Guiseppe Tucci, *Theory and Practice of the Mandala* (London: Rider, 1960); Mircea Eliade, *Yoga: Freedom and Immortality* (New York: Bollingen Books, 1958), especially pp. 219-227; Lama Govinda, *Foundations of Tibetan Mysticism* (London: Rider, 1960); also by Govinda is a book of meditations, reflections and drawings entitled *Mandala: der heilige Kreis* (Zurich: Origo Verlag, 1960); John Blofeld, *The Tantric Mysticism of Tibet* (New York: E.P. Dutton, 1970), especially chapter IV, "Psychic and Material Symbols," pp. 94-125; and Ajit Mookerjee, *Tantra Art: Its Physics and Philosophy* (Paris: Ravi Kumar & New York: Random House, 1968).

Related in form and intention to the Mandalas of the Orient are the American Indian sandpaintings of the Southwest. Again, no formal study has been done relating the two traditions. A basic text is: David Villaseñor, *Tapestries in Sand: The Spirit of Indian Sandpainting* (Healdsburg: Naturegraph Press, 1966), which is most excellent, for it is a "firsthand" account. Other references include: Mary C. Wheelwright, *Beautyway: A Navaho Ceremonial* (New York: Pantheon Books, 1957); Gladys A. Reichard, *Navaho Religion, A Study in*

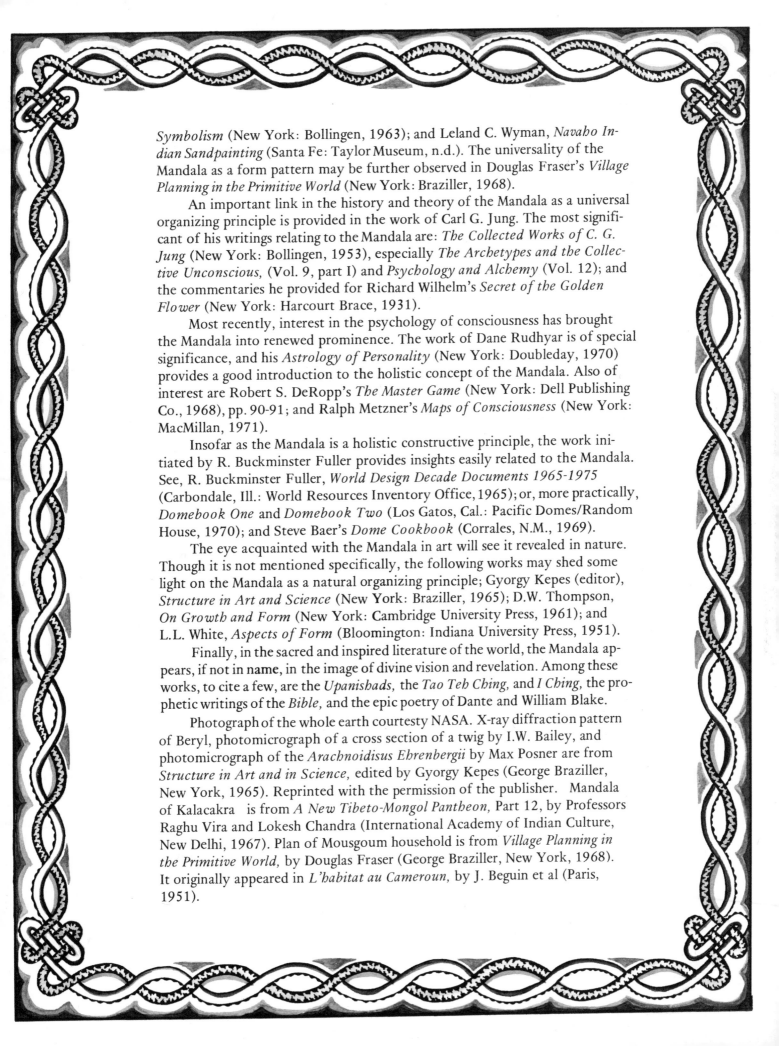

Symbolism (New York: Bollingen, 1963); and Leland C. Wyman, *Navaho Indian Sandpainting* (Santa Fe: Taylor Museum, n.d.). The universality of the Mandala as a form pattern may be further observed in Douglas Fraser's *Village Planning in the Primitive World* (New York: Braziller, 1968).

An important link in the history and theory of the Mandala as a universal organizing principle is provided in the work of Carl G. Jung. The most significant of his writings relating to the Mandala are: *The Collected Works of C. G. Jung* (New York: Bollingen, 1953), especially *The Archetypes and the Collective Unconscious,* (Vol. 9, part I) and *Psychology and Alchemy* (Vol. 12); and the commentaries he provided for Richard Wilhelm's *Secret of the Golden Flower* (New York: Harcourt Brace, 1931).

Most recently, interest in the psychology of consciousness has brought the Mandala into renewed prominence. The work of Dane Rudhyar is of special significance, and his *Astrology of Personality* (New York: Doubleday, 1970) provides a good introduction to the holistic concept of the Mandala. Also of interest are Robert S. DeRopp's *The Master Game* (New York: Dell Publishing Co., 1968), pp. 90-91; and Ralph Metzner's *Maps of Consciousness* (New York: MacMillan, 1971).

Insofar as the Mandala is a holistic constructive principle, the work initiated by R. Buckminster Fuller provides insights easily related to the Mandala. See, R. Buckminster Fuller, *World Design Decade Documents 1965-1975* (Carbondale, Ill.: World Resources Inventory Office, 1965); or, more practically, *Domebook One* and *Domebook Two* (Los Gatos, Cal.: Pacific Domes/Random House, 1970); and Steve Baer's *Dome Cookbook* (Corrales, N.M., 1969).

The eye acquainted with the Mandala in art will see it revealed in nature. Though it is not mentioned specifically, the following works may shed some light on the Mandala as a natural organizing principle; Gyorgy Kepes (editor), *Structure in Art and Science* (New York: Braziller, 1965); D.W. Thompson, *On Growth and Form* (New York: Cambridge University Press, 1961); and L.L. White, *Aspects of Form* (Bloomington: Indiana University Press, 1951).

Finally, in the sacred and inspired literature of the world, the Mandala appears, if not in name, in the image of divine vision and revelation. Among these works, to cite a few, are the *Upanishads,* the *Tao Teh Ching,* and *I Ching,* the prophetic writings of the *Bible,* and the epic poetry of Dante and William Blake.

Photograph of the whole earth courtesy NASA. X-ray diffraction pattern of Beryl, photomicrograph of a cross section of a twig by I.W. Bailey, and photomicrograph of the *Arachnoidisus Ehrenbergii* by Max Posner are from *Structure in Art and in Science,* edited by Gyorgy Kepes (George Braziller, New York, 1965). Reprinted with the permission of the publisher. Mandala of Kalacakra is from *A New Tibeto-Mongol Pantheon,* Part 12, by Professors Raghu Vira and Lokesh Chandra (International Academy of Indian Culture, New Delhi, 1967). Plan of Mousgoum household is from *Village Planning in the Primitive World,* by Douglas Fraser (George Braziller, New York, 1968). It originally appeared in *L'habitat au Cameroun,* by J. Beguin et al (Paris, 1951).

I Am the Mandala
of the Light Eye Give

II

The Mandala as a Visual Process

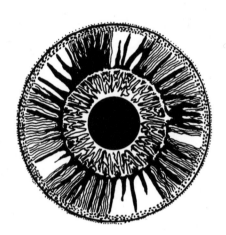

It is first of all necessary to make the organ of vision analogous and similar to the object to be contemplated. Never would the eye have perceived the sun if it had not first taken the form of the sun; likewise, the soul cannot see beauty unless it first becomes beautiful itself, and every man must make himself beautiful and divine in order to attain the sight of beauty and divinity.

Plotinus

The Mandala is fundamentally a visual construct which is easily grasped by the eye, for it corresponds to the primary visual experience as well as to the structure of the organ of sight. The pupil of the eye itself is a simple Mandala form. The eye receives light and projects its images outward through the form of the pupil, that is, through the center of an elementary circle.

The purest, simplest, yet most encompassing form is the circle; the most rudimentary, yet ever-evolving experience of living organisms is that of light, the visible source of which is the sun. A definite relationship exists between the shape and function of the sun, the organ of sight, and the experience of light. The eye is the human intermediary between the gift of outer light and the light that burns within. According to Matthew, Christ said "The eye is the light of the body; if, therefore, thine eye be single, thy whole body shall be full of light." The Mandala can be described as a symbol or vehicle of the process described by Christ whereby the eye is made *single,* like a lens, flooding the organism with light—not the light of the sun but the inner light of which the sun seems but a reflection. Some Taoist teachings state that the eye is the *positive* element whereas the rest of the body is *negative*. In the positive singleness of the eye, in the one-pointedness of this vision, is there not an intimation of the third eye, the all-seeing eye which never sleeps?

Could men see clearly—as the *seers* have always *seen*—there would be no need for Mandalas because experience would be apprehended as an organic whole, continually proceeding from and returning to the one source—the center of being. To *see* is to see the whole of one's experience, and to *know.* The books of the ancient seers of India are called the *Vedas,* a Sanskrit term that relates both to *vis*ion and *wis*dom. For the knowledge of the ancient

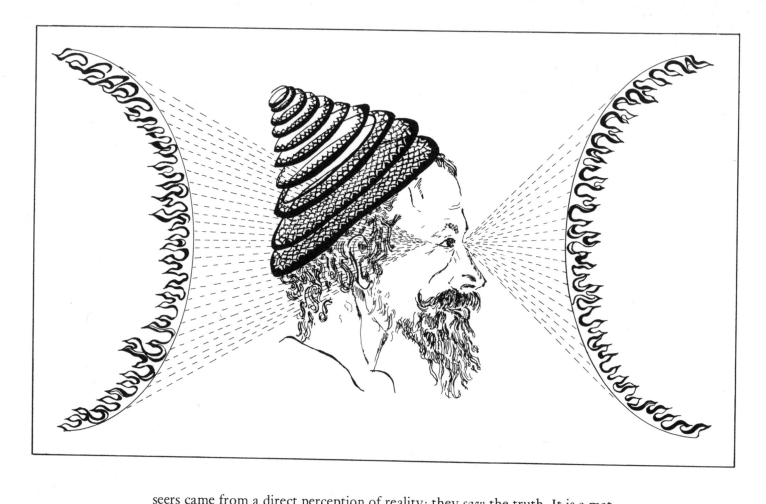

seers came from a direct perception of reality; they *saw* the truth. It is a matter of speculation whether this was because their cultural situation was less sophisticated and less encumbered with perceptual data than ours, thus permitting a greater opportunity for seeing directly, or because they had access to a higher teaching or techniques, or both. In time, with the greater accumulation of perceptual data, direct vision became more difficult to come by, and hence the Mandala was developed as a *reminder* of the direct perception of reality.

The biopsychic nature of the Mandala has been defined:

[The] mechanism of the mandala can also be understood in terms of the neurophysiology of the eye. . . [as] the mandala is a depiction of the structure of the eye, the center of the mandala corresponds to the foeval "blind spot." Since the "blind spot" is the exit from the eye to the visual system of the brain, by going "out" through the center, you are going in to the brain. The Yogin finds the mandala in his own body. The mandala is an instrument for transcending the world of visually perceived phenomena by first centering them and turning them inward.
Ralph Metzner and Timothy Leary

Plate 1: *Golden Egg.* Roberto Matiello.

Plate 2: *Fire in Solomon's Seal.* Henry Sultan.

Plate 3:
Mandala of Evolution.
Dion Wright.

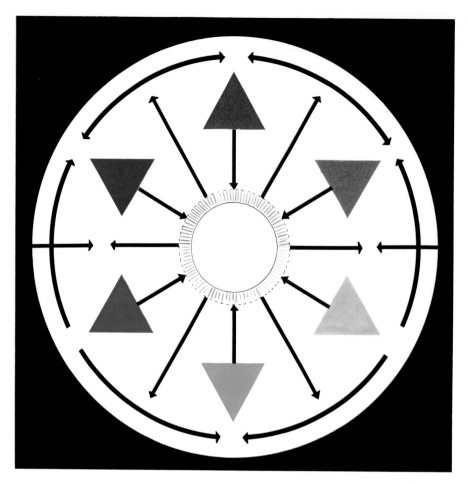

Plate 4: *Color Wheel.*

Plate 5: *Mandala.* Jeanette Stobie.

A direct means of recovering the Mandala is through simple visual exercises and observations regarding one's own visual apparatus and processes. For instance, observe the pattern of the retina by gently pressing on the closed eyelids. Reflect on the nature and intensity of the light that accompanies these patterns, for surely there is little darkness here, though the eyes have no direct access to the sun. Concentration with the eyes closed is an excellent means for de-conditioning the eye and brain. Seeing and perceiving all-too-automatically is often the case with culturally over-sophisticated individuals. Closing the eyes, letting go, and then observing what happens is a good exercise, if only to realize how incessant is the torrent of thoughts and images (whether or not these images are actually "visualized"). It is often beneficial to introduce *concentration objects* in order to center this chaotic profusion of data.

It is not necessary that the concentrator actually *see* the objects, but that he have a mental construct of them. The following is a simple progression that can be studied, and then, with eyes closed, concentrated upon, first recreating the entire progression, and then holding the progression as a simultaneous entirety:

In doing such an exercise, proceed slowly. Often it is easier to concentrate on abstract forms if some kind of "story" accompanies the imagery. If this is so, allow the "story" or narrative to be spontaneously created. Ideally, the preceding visual progression would suggest some kind of cosmogenesis or cosmic process.

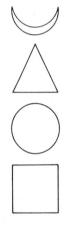 Another progression can be mentally reconstructed in much the same manner as the previous series. Here, the progression is vertical, moving from the bottom to the top. A suggested narrative or set of associations is that of the elements: square—earth; crescent—water; triangle—fire; and circle—air. Explore and feel the various forms; note what, if any, inner body associations correspond to the suggested form symbols. In using the elemental associations, try to see how these structures are appropriate to the elements. Or, mentally concentrate upon each of the four elements, and then see what, if any, forms suggest themselves.

While using an inner narrative as an aid in holding and creating these images in the mind's eye, attempt to maintain a state of detached awareness. Other forms may suggest themselves or grow out of the forms concentrated upon. These forms and the progressions they engender may be noted, but the visualization process should not be "interrupted." *Do not try to hold on,* just observe and let go, for the most important factor is to stimulate as spontaneous a process as possible. Only from this spontaneous flow, and in this flow, does creativity arise. Much practice is needed before a person can penetrate beneath the culturally conditioned levels of response and attain with ease the level of the spontaneous flow. There is no need to worry that anything will be "lost"—whatever has been "seen" has come from the source, and the source is within.

 In the process of these elementary concentration exercises, colors may have been perceived. These colors are not necessarily related to any specific image but may appear as simple, ever-changing, abstract color fields in themselves. Here you may ask, where did this color—or these colors—come from? If you have difficulty in visualizing form, color is usually much simpler to experience. Form is the most complicated aspect of the process of visual perception; it is also the most abstract. What the eye initially perceives are not forms, but light. Pure light is much too intense, and is decomposed into color in order to be perceived.

Just as the Mandala is basically a simple form or series of forms, so are the colors that are used in classical Mandalas such as the Tibetan, or Southwest Indian sandpaintings—simple and symbolic in nature. For our purpose, the basic colors are red, orange, yellow, green, blue, and violet. These are the spectral or prismatic colors. In addition, there are black and white which are often not considered as colors. This is by no means to limit the choice, but it is best to begin as simply as possible. Furthermore, the eye reacts more readily to the pure, simple colors.

The six colors we have listed can be arranged into a simple Mandala so that their relationships can be more fully grasped (see Plate 4). In our arrangement we are stressing the complementariness or polarity of the different colors. White, which is the combination or simultaneous experience of all the spectral colors—recalling Newton's experiment with the prism—is diffused from the center. White is pure light; it is within, radiating outward. Black is outside of our construction. Black is the "lack" of color; it is without; it is the primal chaos. The six spectral colors are arranged in the form of a six-pointed star—two interpenetrating equilateral triangles. The angles of the upward-pointing triangle symbolize the "primary" colors: red, yellow, and blue. The three angles of the downward-pointing triangle represent the three "secondary" colors. Each of the secondary colors is composed of the two primaries on either side of it: red and yellow combined make orange; blue and red make violet; and yellow and blue make green. The secondary, spectral colors in turn may be combined with the adjacent primaries to produce the tertiary gradations of hues. Ideally, the circumference joining the points of the star contains all the gradations of the six colors as they pass into each other.

The six colors are arranged so that each falls opposite its complementary. The complementaries are: red (primary) and green (secondary); blue (primary) and orange (secondary); yellow (primary) and violet (secondary). Any two complementary hues placed adjacent to each other create a clash or visual flash effect; when mixed they tend to cancel each other out and produce a grayish-white effect. Any set of complementaries comprises the three primary colors whose light-wave fusion is white. For example, the complementary pair, red-and-green, is composed of the primary color, red, and the secondary color, green, which is the combination of the other two primaries, blue and yellow. There is also the complementary after-image effect: stare at a color for a few moments, and then look away or close the eyes; the after-image will appear as the complementary of the original color. The complementaries define each other immediately as a matter of consciousness, such as the *yin* and *yang* reveal their mutual interdependence in the *t'ai chi* symbol. Technically this is known as the law of simultaneous contrast.

The perception of color is subjective and is as much an internal visual phenomenon as an external one. Red is often thought of as a warm, passionate color—blue as a much calmer, cooler color. Every individual associates different emotional and subjective values with different colors, and there is no absolute one-to-one correlation between color and subjective value. This being so, contemplate the diagram and discover what associations and emotional reactions the colors evoke. Consider the directions of the compass—North, South, East, and West, as well as the center—and attribute specific colors to each of these

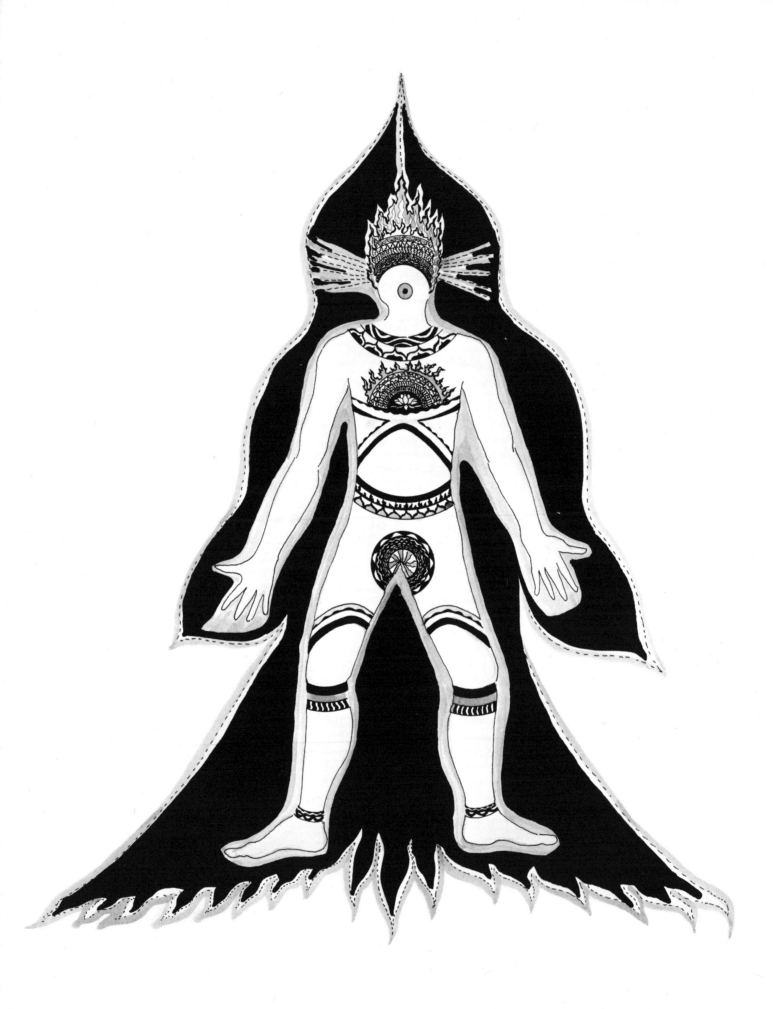

directions. Various Native American and Oriental cultures associate colors with the different directions as an integral feature of their Mandalas of orientation.

Corresponding to the association of color and direction is that of specific colors with different parts of the body, much as different colors are related to the various emotional dispositions and temperaments. Lying down with eyes closed, visualize the various parts and/or functions of the body in terms of specific colors. What color is the head or mental zone? What color is the throat, the zone of speech? the lungs and the breathing function? the heart and circulatory function? the spine? the digestive area? the sex and eliminative organs? the limbs of the body? Do not force the visualization of the color, rather focus on specific areas or functions and see which, if any, color may appear or suggest itself.

As an exercise of inner visualization, consider the spectral colors as radiating out from the heart, much in the manner of the color diagram. With the heart as a center of pure white light, imagine a circular rainbow slowly filling the entire body. Let the head be the apex of the upward pointing triangle, the point of scintillating violet/red light. Then imagine the extremities of the body as describing the points of a circle. The circumference is described by an imaginary line that connects the head to the extended left hand to the left foot, to the right foot, to the extended right hand, and back again to the head. Within this circular body-field, the left side becomes filled with the red-to-orange-to-yellow-to-green color zone. The corresponding color zone of the right side of the body flows from green-to-blue-to-violet-to-red.

Imagine these colors filling the body, work slowly, feel the color as energy permeating every cell of your body, extending outward in every direction from the heart, until you are a pulsing, surging, circular rainbow, radiant with color and full of peace. As the color flows out from the center it becomes darker in hue and cooler in temperature as it reaches the outer circumference of the body field.

When dealing with exercises emphasizing the color zones of the body, the question of the aura, or body-field, naturally arises. Without getting involved in technical questions regarding the existence or nonexistence of the aura, it is a good exercise to extend the color field with which you have filled your body to the area surrounding your body. Concentrate on the body-boundary. Relax your sense of body definition. Allow the colors that fill a particular area to extend and filter out beyond the area of the body. If you wish, imagine these extra-corporeal extensions as ultra-violet (or ultra-blue or -red or -green). Ultra-violet and the other "ultras" are the colors of the spectrum invisible to the normal human eye.

Try to have some sense of the circular rainbow radiating out from the heart center to the extremities and to the field beyond the circumference of the body; hold it there for a short while, letting the energy of the colors pulse and flow. Consider the kinds of feelings, emotions and mental associations that come and go with the colors in the different parts of the body. From where does this color energy flow? What causes it to flow and fill the mental/body field?

Now return the colors to their source, the heart center. Slowly bring the rainbow/prism back, reversing the flow of the color energy streaming forth from the heart. While doing this, try to feel the white light at the center expanding outward so that as the color energies stream back into their source, the source of white light is spreading outward, slowly filling the body with the primal light of experience. The pure white light of undifferentiated being, totally luminous, incandescent, dazzlingly pure, fills the entirety of the body to the point of dissolving, until there is no body, no contour, no body/environmental tension—just the purity of the light, at once the center, self-same for all things and all beings, the one source that lies deep within the very desire to be. Float in it as it dissolves the impurities and purifies the elements.

Immersed in this all-pervasive light, realize this is the light of primal experience, immanent in all things. The "distortions" of perceptual and cultural conditioning impede the pure experience of this light. What or who is seeing this light? Which eyes have seen this experience? Are these the eyes of flesh or the eyes of fire?

There is something that feeds the sun, visible only to the eyes of fire, for if the eyes of flesh were to gaze upon it but for a moment, they would melt and wither at the very glance. This in-visible light/energy is available to us as it is to the sun, for we cannot exist without it anymore than the sun, should its source go out.

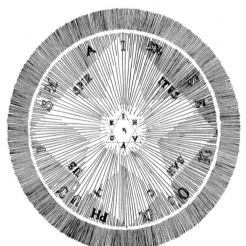

Life is a pure flame
and we live
as if by an invisible sun
burning within us.

Sir Thomas Brown
The Urn Burial

Whatever science has been able to tell us of the eyes of flesh, it has been less certain in speaking of the inner visual capacities. Whether called memory, dream, prevision, clairvoyance, hallucination, or intuition, there is no satisfactory answer to the causes and qualities of these phenomena. The greatest insight, thought, and art concerning the human condition and its divine aspirations are rooted in the phenomenon of inner vision. The tradition of the Perennial Philosophy speaks of the third eye, the eye above and between the eyes of flesh. It is this eye to which Christ refers, and which, in the Hindu tradition, is called the *Ajña*, the eye of wisdom, or the eye of knowledge.

The third eye is often symbolized by a double-petalled lotus, which may also be viewed as the infinity sign. ∞ This convention readily denotes the quality of the two eyes of the body drawn together seeing no longer separately and finitely, but unitively and in-finitely. In the Yogic tradition this state is described as *ekagrata:* one-pointedness. It is the capacity of seeing from the center of the self, of being that center, moving always from the same center, no matter how much things may change.

This is the vision of the eye of the Mandala. Go to the center and know the Whole. Follow this path. Turn inward and see with the eyes of fire the Mandala that is the Whole—I am the Mandala of the Light Eye give—this is the Path of Fire.

Voyagers of the light
    Blooming from the seed of light
    Blown into the space of eternal dawn...
Chanting the one remembrance:
For that is the path that leads beyond
Forever, forever beyond, beyond
Knowing only that invisible force
Of which our bodies
Are the fragmentary rainbow reflection
O let us move on
Like a wind
        Blowing through the sun!

Notes

An excellent summary study on the nature of the eye and visual perception is R.L. Gregory, *Eye and Brain: The Psychology of Seeing* (New York: McGraw-Hill, 1966). Relationship of the eye to the Mandala is discussed in the work of Ralph Metzner and Timothy Leary, "On Programming Psychedelic Experiences," *Psychedelic Review,* No. 9, 1967, pp. 4-19. The function and nature of color has been successfully explored by Faber Birren in numerous writings, two of which we mention here: *Color Psychology and Color Therapy* (New Hyde Park: University Books, 1961); and *Color: A Survey in Words and Pictures* (New Hyde Park; University Books, 1963).

The more subjective phenomena of vision which relate to the theory and nature of the Mandala are investigated and described in Annie Besant and C. W. Leadbeatter, *Thought Forms* (Wheaton: The Theosophical Publishing House, 1967); and Edwin Babbit, *Principles of Light and Color* (New Hyde Park: University Books, 1967). Christ's famous pronouncements on inner vision are from Matthew, VI, 22. For more information on the nature of inner vision according to some of the esoteric traditions we suggest Lu K'uan Yu, *Taoist Yoga: Alchemy and Immortality* (New York: Samuel Weiser, 1970); Sir John Woodroffe, *The Serpent Power* (Madras: Ganesh & Co., 1964), and José Argüelles, *Charles Henry and the Formation of a Psychophysical Aesthetic* (Chicago: University of Chicago Press, 1972).

Illustration on page 30 is from *A Christian Rosenkreutz Anthology,* compiled and edited by Paul M. Allen (Rudolf Steiner Publications, Blauvelt, New York, 1968).

According to the Sacred and

Magical Art: I Am That

32

III

The Mandala as Art Form

Every being
  entering into the ineffable sanctuary of its own nature
  finds there a symbol of the
Father of All. Proclus

The Mandala has appeared throughout man's history as a universal and essential symbol of integration, harmony, and transformation. It gives form to the most primordial intuition of the nature of reality, an intuition that inheres in each of us, giving us life.

The circle is the original sign, the prime symbol of the nothing and the all; the symbol of heaven and the solar eye, the all-encompassing form beyond and through which man finds and loses himself. This is the originless Mandala. No race is without it, for it comprises the All, its source and its ending. It is the center of the Hawaiian Cross of the Flower of the Sun, from which stream forth the eight solar deities. This Solar Flower was associated with the creative principle, *Tane*, "The Lord who radiated reddish-gold rays of sunlight." From this description is derived one of the titles of the Creator: *Tane of the magnificent cross of light!* Although a fiery creative principle, the center of this deity, symbolized by the solar flower, is described as a fountainhead from which flows the Living Water of Life.

Sunrise at Stonehenge.

The Mandala is the symbol of the round of life and death, of the cosmic procession of beings, planets and stars, of earthly seasons and galactic cycles. In this spirit the Druids of ancient England, before the coming of the Romans, constructed the monument of Stonehenge. This massive concentricity consists essentially of two circles: the inner or Sarsen circle, which originally contained thirty upright stones; and the outer, or circle of the Trilithins, fifty-six in number. Both of these circles contained passageways between each of the individual stones. Viewed from the center of this complex, these passages created definite angles through which the movements of the stars and heavenly bodies could be seen, followed, measured and venerated. As has recently been observed, Stonehenge is not only a colossal megalithic structure commemorating some primeval conception of the solar and life forces, nor simply a temple for the enactment of certain rituals. Were Stonehenge the composite of these religio-aesthetic functions, it would be magnificent enough. But it was also the basic feature and landmark of the knowledge systematized by the Druids, for it served as a calendar and astronomical guide. In the words of Gerald Hawkins, Stonehenge may be thought of as a "neolithic computer."

The integration of worship, knowledge, and beauty is a significant feature of the Mandala, enabling it to convey a teaching to the receptive. Mandalas correspond to Ouspensky's idea of "objective" works of art. Such art expresses a knowledge of the laws of harmony. It is not concerned with the personal, but with the transpersonal; not with the fugitive and the arbitrary, but with the eternal. The "transpersonal" man acts as the agent both of those energies which comprise and define his earthly existence, and those energies beyond him— whether these are called cosmic radiations, soul forces, or divine emanations. These creative forces pour *through man* the "fuel" that vitalizes his life, much as the energies of the sun supply the earth with its life-sustaining capabilities. Transpersonal art, of which the Mandala is an example, is not an end in itself, but a transmitting agent, a lens focusing the higher energies.

34

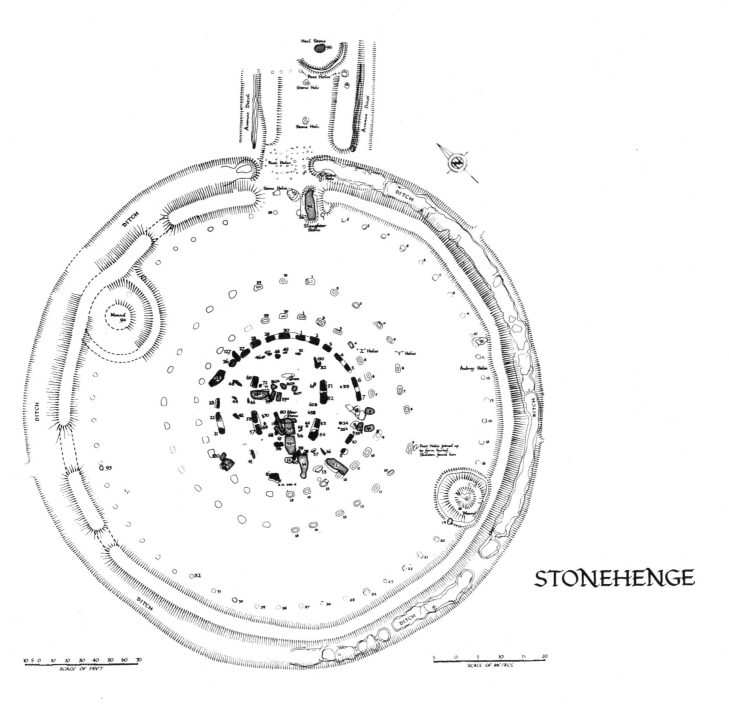

STONEHENGE

Art serves beauty. . . . *Just as soon as art begins to take delight in
that beauty which is already* found, *instead of* the search for new
beauty, *an arrestment occurs and art becomes a superfluous
estheticism, encompassing man's vision like a wall. The aim of art is
the search for beauty, just as the aim of religion is the search for
God and truth. And exactly as art stops, so religion stops also as
soon as it ceases to search for God and truth, thinking it has found
them. This idea is expressed in the precept: ". . . Seek the Kingdom
of God and His Righteousness. . . " It does not say find, but merely
seek!*

P.D. Ouspensky

No two Mandalas are ever the same; for every different locale, the form
and tradition develops in its own unique way, in accordance with the patterns
of ever-evolving nature. Occasionally a monument such as Stonehenge is produced, expressing at every level the cycle of alternating rhythms comprising
the whole of the experience of both space and time as an inseparable cultural
unity.

The cosmogeny, calendar and metaphysical history of the ancient Mexicans is concentrated in one powerful image: the famed Aztec Sunstone. Eleven feet, two inches in diameter and weighing twenty-four and one-half tons, the Sunstone has as its center the symbol of the present fifth age—*Ollin*—symmetrically framing the symbols of the previous four ages. Radiating out from the central symbol are a series of circles representing twenty different day signs which occur repeatedly and are the constants of the Mexican calendar system. This band of signs is surrounded next by a band of celestial symbols signifying light, strength, and beauty. The outermost circle contains two celestial fire serpents, symbolizing the meeting of the two polar forces of the cosmos: light and darkness. Their struggle and continual encounter causes everything in the universe to come into being. On a mundane level this corresponds to the endless alternation of day and night.

According to the sages of *Anahuac* ("Surrounded by Water"—the Nahuatl term for Mexico), in each age an entire race of men was created, developed, and then destroyed. The folly of man initiated a cataclysm symbolized by one each of the four elements—earth, air, fire and water—which climaxed each of these ages. The Aztecs, the last cultural wave of the races of *Anahuac*, conceived of their era as the fifth age. They believed this age would come to a close in the near future in another great cataclysm, symbolized by the sign *Ollin* which means earth-shaking, change, and movement: *the time of the great transition.* After this event, presumably, an entire new cycle of ages would begin.

The theory of the ages of man is a Mandala common to human culture. The Mediterranean progression from the Golden through the Silver and Bronze to the present Iron Age is similar to the Hindu Yugas: Satya, Dwarpara, Treta and Kali. The first age of each cycle is believed to be the longest and most virtuous; each succeeding age increasingly degenerates, and decreases in duration. At the end of an entire cycle of ages occurs a period of great disintegration and transformation. These considerations indicate the cosmic scope and depth to which the Mandala form naturally lends itself. From whichever point a Mandala is entered, a path opens that leads to the eternal center.

The ability to know the beginning of antiquity
is called the thread running through the way.
Lao Tzu

The Australian Tjuringa stone—revealed to youths at the time of the great initiation of puberty—serves basically as a map recalling the origin of all things and bears the title, "Map of the Journeying of the Ancestors of the Dream-Time." The Dream-Time is Eternity, the Ancestors are those beings or states of being through and by which all that we see, know, and experience becomes possible. To find one's way back to the Dream-Time, as the map indicates, is to return to the eternal center. From this center the Ancestors within every man weave their webs and spin their tales. The stone is literally used in telling stories as the storyteller traces the lines with his finger from the center outward. It is like a phonograph record: the man's finger the needle, and his voice the speaker system. Because of this process, many Tjuringa stone designs develop as spiral forms.

With its eight cardinal points—and a ninth, the center point—the Tjuringa stone, reproduced here, recalls the eight petals of the Solar Flower of the Hawaiians, or the Eight-fold Wheel of the Law, the *Dharmachakra* of the Buddhists. In this Tjuringa stone, however, the eight cardinal points are not joined together by a circle, but rather a cross.

The cross introduces another Mandala form-variant, the square. According to Jung, the circle symbolizes essentially the processes of nature or the cosmos as a whole, while the square refers to the universe as conceived and projected by man. The circle represents both the subconscious and the superconscious aspects of nature, whereas the square is related to the conscious rational aspects. In their integration these two represent a holistic world view.

Originating from the center point of the primordial Mandala, the cross defines the four cardinal points of the compass. When connected, these four points form a square or diamond shape.

This is the essential shape of the God's eye of the contemporary Peyote cults of Mexico. The Eyes are made by placing two sticks at right angles so that

Mandala of the Ages.

they form a cross. Various colored threads are then wound around the sticks beginning at the center and worked out toward the ends or cardinal points to create a diamond/square shape about the skeletal cross. This simple design affords a beautiful and instructive example in the nature of the Mandala as an artistic process.

The cross as a universal symbol appears in nearly all cultures, attesting to the structural identity of the human mind and its creative expressions. The swastika, as a variant of the cross, is equally widespread, common to the New World and the Old. Often associated with the idea of motion or change, it signifies the path of the sun setting in motion the four cardinal points—North, South, East, and West—giving rise to the phenomenon of the seasons. In the swastika and the cross, with whatever particulars they may be associated, the key notion is the relation of the four points to the center and through the center to each other. Hence the symbolic meaning of the crossroads: that place in which all things are met and from which all things are possible.

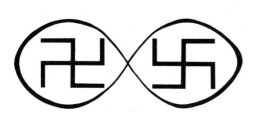

The center of the swastika is the symbol of the Great Spirit, the Great Mystery, from which all things emanate.

David Villaseñor

As the basic symbol of the Christian religion, the cross takes much of its significance from the conception of the crossroads. Christ, as the mystical symbol of the spiritual potential inherent in men, derives His meaning from the cross. When He declares, "He who would follow me must take up his own cross. . .", He is alluding to the significance of the crossroads, asking men to enter into the center of their own being so that they may take a new direction. A common image of Christ depicts him as the *center* of a halo or radiating auric field, His majestic personal emanations vibrating outward from the body: "Christ in Glory." Around Christ are placed representations or symbols of the Four Apostles: Matthew, Mark, Luke and John, whose symbolic forms are respectively: Angel (or man), Lion, Ox, and Eagle. These figures are usually placed at a 45° angle to Christ. In certain traditions these four positions are termed the Gates of the Avatars or the Divine Manifestations, that is, the pathways leading to the central avataric symbol, in this case, Christ.

Perhaps the most characteristic Christian symbol using the mandaloid form of the cross is Christ crucified. Here the element of sacrifice is associated with the center principle. Christ, as one of the most profound symbols of sacrifice, expresses the return to the center and the stripping away, the yielding of personal artifice, ambition, and ego. What is given up in the act of sacrifice is attachment to worldly attainment, including, in the case of Christ, the body itself. The cross also symbolizes the *tree of life:* only by dying to itself, by submitting to the inevitable forces of decay and disintegration and returning to the center is the tree able to grow beyond itself, even if this "beyond" is but a mere seed once more fallen to the earth. The Cross becomes the harbinger of the seed.

Labyrinth in Chartres Cathedral.

All that is visible must grow beyond itself, extend into the realm of the invisible. Thereby it receives its true consecration and clarity and takes firm root in the cosmic order.

"The Cauldron", I Ching

In a sculpture from the ancient Mayan city, Palenque, the cross is a symbol of the tree of life growing out of a figure who has sacrificed himself. In sacrifice nothing is lost, rather something is transfigured or transformed into an aspect beyond the original configuration, much as matter is transformed into energy. In either case, passage occurs through the mysterious center of things.

The Medieval Christian symbols or the Cross of Palenque are not to be considered as separate works of art, but have to be understood within the context of the larger sacred structures which they help to articulate and beautify. In one sense, all sacred religious structures partake of the Mandala principle: the Egyptian and Mexican pyramids; the temples of India; Buddhist stupas; Islamic mosques; the pagodas of China and Japan; and the tipis and kivas of North America. The most highly developed cruciform Mandala is in the churches and cathedrals of the Christian World. In Medieval Europe the very structure and environment of the Christian church took on a primary Mandala cross shape. The Greek and Byzantine churches had developed a perfect cruciform with a dome center.

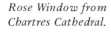

Rose Window from Chartres Cathedral.

The churches of the later Romanesque and Gothic West acquired the form of an elongated, or Latin cross, as it later came to be called. The significant spot is the altar at the center of the cross: everything is oriented to this point. The major churches were literally oriented to the East, the place of the sunrise and resurrection. These cathedrals, and Hindu temples of the same period, were the repository of the teachings of their respective cultures: carved in stone on the exterior and interior; painted where paint would take; and, in the case of the Gothic cathedrals, illumined in blazing light through stained glass windows. These "rose windows" form some of the finest organic circular Mandalas created by man.

Palenque Stone.

43

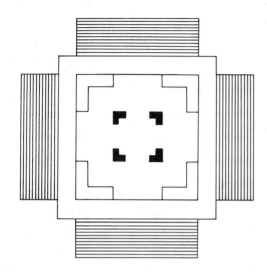

The Gothic cathedrals of the thirteenth century mark the last major phase of an attempt at creating an integrated, highly centered, cultural complex in the European West. These temple complexes are a part of a highpoint of a planetary wave of human culture. Despite geographical isolation, a unitary human purpose, design and meaning becomes apparent in the erection of cathedrals, mosques, and temples in the general period of the tenth through fifteenth centuries: Kajuraho in India; Borobadur in Java; Ankor Wat in Indochina; Chartres in France; Córdoba in Islamic Spain; and Chichen Itza in Yucatan. The world view which these edifices have in common is that each man is a cosmic unit and that the society in which he lives is a reflection of a map of the cosmos.

Whether called sacred art or objective art, the Mandala is a form of magic. In speaking of magic we refer to a fundamental process—a willed, conscious action. Art as magic serves its supreme function when it leads an entire collectitivity into a new realm of consciousness. Abbot Suger of Saint-Denis in the twelfth century spoke of the "anagogical" function of the stained glass windows which he had introduced into the previously austere church environment. By anagogical Suger meant that which leads the senses through contemplation to a state beyond the senses. When man's creative actions and art forms are capable of doing just this, we are no longer dealing with art but with magic. And that magic is all the greater and more powerful which involves and is the participatory creation of an entire community. Such is the case with the Gothic cathedrals, the finest rugs of Afghanistan, and the ritual observances of those people in tune with the creative forces of nature. When this relationship has been broken or concealed, we are dealing with another form of magic, the magic of the wizards of darkness.

The magic of the Mandala is derived from its attunement to the creative forces, expressed and embodied in the very fabric of everyday life: through the Mandala man lives as a cosmic citizen.

In the European West, art as a form of collective participatory magic dies out by the sixteenth century. Magical art survives in the West after the sixteenth century only as an adjunct to alchemy and the increasingly underground "occult" sciences. With the rise of scientific rationalism in the seventeenth century, the Mandala principle fades from the screen of the conscious collective activities of the West. From this time on, Western artistic and aesthetic principles and practices adopt an increasingly scientific, rational attitude. From the point of view of the Mandala, this approach is detrimental to the health of the organism as a whole: such a strict rationalism excludes more and more the possibility of integration with nonrational faculties. Magical art is predicated precisely upon the participatory integration of the various levels or stages of consciousness.

The process of history is itself a Mandala, in which the unfolding drama of the forces of light and darkness find in the cyclic vicissitudes of the races of men the screen upon which the energy of the cosmic struggles may be projected. In the West, the rise of a rational and seemingly anti-magical art and and consciousness in itself is magic. It is as if the mirror of unity which the cathedral builders had shown to European man had been broken and dissolved. But what European man had done in the breaking of this mirror had inevitable planetary consequences, for in the destruction of the mirror of unitive vision, demonic energies were unleashed, energies that would not be satisfied until every last unitive mirror in the world had been broken, or at least concealed by the smoke of wrathful and acquisitive powers.

It is difficult to objectively evaluate what has happened as a result of the European expansion which marked the beginning of the present era; yet very gradually a global perspective is forming. Man's conscious activities must be seen in light of a larger ecological fabric and in relation to the biosphere, atmosphere, and other levels or layers which form the evolving matrix of the planet earth. Man shapes and is shaped by forces of the planet.

MOTTO

Make a circle out of a man and a woman, out of this a square,
   out of this a triangle,
make a circle and you will have the Philosopher's Stone.

EPIGRAM

Make a circle out of a man and a woman,
From which a quadrangular body arises with equal sides,
Derive from it a triangle, which is in contact on all sides with a
   round sphere:
Then the Stone will have come into existence.
If such a great thing is not immediately clear in your mind
Then know, that you will understand everything, if you
   understand the theory of Geometry.

It is no coincidence that the first major European wave of world expansion began in 1519, when Cortes, under the banner of the cross, landed on the eastern shores of Mexico. This landing coincided to the very day with the ancient Mexican prophecies which stated that 1519 would be the point at which the powers of light—Quetzalcoatl, the plumed serpent—were to be superseded by the powers of darkness—Tezcatlipoca, which significantly enough means "smoking mirror." From this date was to follow a period of nine fifty-two-year-long hell periods, which would last until 1987. From the point of view of the global Mandala, there is much power and truth in these facts. The destruction of the Mexican people and their culture—degenerate as certain of the features of their civilization had become—can be considered the paradigm of the encounters between the modern European and the rest of the peoples and cultures of the world.

Gradually, the unitive traditions of the various people of the earth slowly succumbed to the onslaught of the smoking mirror. In India and much of Asia, a process of infiltration and sabotage completed the task; in Africa, wholesale enslavement; in America, genocide and disease—and everywhere the twin nemeses of economic and psychological exploitation. The living traditions have been turned into museum pieces, and in one sense the world has become a massive graveyard where Shiva, the god of destruction and transformation, performs a mighty dance. This entire process finds a parallel metaphor in the traditions of the sandpainted Mandalas of the American Southwest: when the Mandala serving one specific purpose and occasion has been completed, it is erased and destroyed, but only that another one may be created.

Vajrapani.

The last of the unitive mirrors was broken when Tibet fell to the conquering armies of a new, rationalized China in 1959. Significantly, the Tibetans were the last cultural stronghold where the art of the Mandala was practiced at a level of power, complexity, and beauty, perhaps unparalleled in any other culture of the globe. The Mandala is now free to be reborn anywhere on the planet—to begin a new cycle of development. And this, too, is part of the magic, the completing and raising to a higher level of consciousness an entire phase of human development: history as a mandalic process.

If the art of magic can be read in history, the process we have been describing is the disintegration of one Mandala, the dissolution of one developmental phase of consciousness back to the center point. The various regional expressions of the sacred art of the globe have been more or less destroyed, only to be created anew at a fuller, more integrative and comprehensive level. This process has been vividly described in the visions of the Sioux holy man, Black Elk, as the breaking of the hoop of his people. Symbolically this is the breaking of the hoop of the Mandala of all the races of man in the present era. In Black Elk's vision, the hoop of his people will be reunited only when the tree of the center flowers once again. This is the vision of a Mandala of global consciousness. The era of disintegration is the age of the profane, of the breaking of the hoop of the peoples, of the destruction of the sacred traditions by

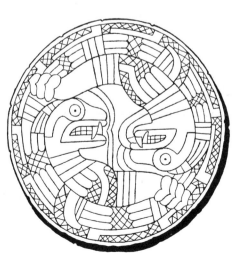

The good painter is wise
God is in his heart
He puts divinity into things
He converses with his own heart.

which man realizes at every moment and in every act his inseparable interrelationship and interdependence with every other creature and thing on earth and in the universe. Among a "sacred" people, everything reflects the simple, yet dynamic ordering principle of creation.

In a profane cultural phase such as the present one, the primordial creative principle of sacred art happens only by chance, or through the unconscious process of dreams or what we call madness and reverie. Yet, by the very magic of the Mandala process, the various elements of consciousness, no matter how disparate, are delivered in the final heaving of chaos to that center or void which is the beginning point of every sacred manifestation.

The unitive vision of the Mandala re-enters through the conflict and tragedy of a planet almost completely polarized. We are at the frontier of a new level of integration. Everything in the world is crying for it. And in this process the principles of sacred art return once more to their rightful place in human development. The Mandala may become once more the root-image of a global symbolism, a common and organic language utterly necessary for unifying the now diverse remnants of what was once a brotherhood.

Before building anew, the previous creation must be dissolved. This is the significance underlying the transformation of the present world Mandala. Applied to the individual, there must be a process of disidentification from the polarities for the purpose of arriving at that primordial point where man can exclaim: I am That! or, in the words of the ancient Vedic seers: Thou art That— *Tat Tvam Asi.* To understand the divine nature of things is to become rooted in the heart of the divine. This is the privilege of man. The ancient Mexicans described the artist/seer as a *Yolteotl, one whose heart is rooted in God.*

Notes

Concerning Sacred or Objective Art: Titus Burckhardt, *Sacred Art in East and West* (London: Perennial Books, 1967); P.D. Ouspensky, *In Search of the Miraculous* (New York: Harcourt, Brace, 1949), especially Chapter 14, pp. 278-98; and by the same author, *Tertium Organum: A Key to the Enigmas of the World* (New York: Vintage Books, 1970), Chapter XVIII, pp. 192-208; Erwin Panofsky, "Abbot Suger of St. Denis," *Meaning in the Visual Arts* (New York: Doubleday, 1957), pp. 108-145; T.C. Stewart, *The City as an Image of Man* (London: Latimer Press, 1970).

Texts dealing with the more specialized areas include: Leinani Melville, *Children of the Rainbow: The Religion, Legends, and Gods of Pre-Christian Hawaii* (Wheaton, Ill.: The Theosophical Publishing Co., 1969); Gerald Hawkins, *Stonehenge Decoded* (New York: Doubleday, 1965); Tony Shearer, *Lord of the Dawn* (Healdsburg, Ca.: Naturegraph Publishers, 1971), and by the same author, *The Sacred Calendar* (Denver: Western News, 1967); Miguel Leon-Portilla, *Aztec Thought and Culture* (Norman: University of Oklahoma, Press, 1963); A.P. Elkin, *The Australian Aborigine* (New York: Doubleday, 1964), especially, Chapter IX, "Art and Ritual," pp. 232-255; Antoinette K. Gordon, *Tibetan Religious Art* (New York: Paragon Books, 1963); the already mentioned *Tapestries in Sand* by David Villaseñor; Heinrich Zimmer, *Myths in Indian Art and Civilization* (Princeton: Princeton University Press, 1946); Giuseppe Tucci, *Tibetan Painted Scrolls* (Rome: Istituto Poligrafica Dello Stato, 1947); Michael Maier, *Atalanta Fugiens,* translated and edited by H.M.E. De Jong (Leiden: E. J. Brill, 1969).

Photograph and plan of Stonehenge are British Crown Copyright—reproduced with the permission of the Controller of HBM Stationery Office. Photograph of the Aztec Calendar Stone courtesy of Instituto Nacional de Anthropologia e Historia, Mexico City. Photograph of the Rose Window from Chartres Cathedral is from *French Cathedrals,* by Jean Bony (Viking Press, New York, 1961). The Palenque Stone is from *A Coloring Book of Ancient Mexico and Peru,* by Karen Olsen Bruhns, designed by Tom Weller (St. Heironymous Press, Berkeley, 1971). The Motto and Epigram accompanying the illustration on page 46 are from Michael Maier's *Atalanta Fugiens,* by H.M.E. De Jong (E.J. Brill, Leiden, 1969). Vajrapani is from *Kalachakra,* compiled by Tarthang Tulku (Dharma Press, Berkeley, 1971).

So That In Me

the Plan Illumined Grows

IV
The Mandala as a Key to Symbolic Systems

...the man who understands a symbol not only "opens himself" to the objective world, but at the same time succeeds in emerging from his personal situation and reaching a comprehension of the universal... Thanks to the symbol, the individual experience is "awoken", and transmuted into a spiritual act. Mircea Eliade

Beyond its inherent and captivating beauty, sacred art is the formal aspect of a system of symbols. Symbols are containers of various levels of knowledge, and relate to far more than what they superficially embody. They are created through a condensation and focalization of energies and, by a reciprocal process, can release those energies. A coherent set of symbols constitutes a symbolic system. These systems are often structured in the form of a Mandala, for they attempt to define the processes of nature as a set of interrelationships unified into a formulable whole.

Since it is the mind of man that realizes and integrates the various parts of a given system, such a system may also be described as a map of consciousness. Consciousness is the power of an organism to order, integrate and transform itself. An organism is an integrated, ongoing, self-contained set of relationships, whether a cell, an individual, a community, or a solar system.

Man's efforts at creating a meaningful way of life in accord with the laws of nature have led to the view of himself as the microcosm. Through contemplating his very form and the nature of his existence, man has often found a correspondence or series or correspondences to the workings of the cosmos as a whole—the macrocosm. This perception is at the base of many symbolic systems. If man conceives of himself as a microcosm, his way of life and community also take on the character of a cosmic order. Inherent in this idea is an intuition of the basic harmony of the universe and of man's desire to realize himself accordingly. If nature is a harmony and man a part of nature, then man himself must be innately harmonic. The laws governing his mind and body reflect and partake of the functioning of greater nature.

Symbolic systems exist to help, develop, maintain, and, if necessary, recover an organic way of life—*the way of developing nature.* In Chinese this is called the *Tao,* which is often translated as "the way." However:

The way that can be told
Is not the constant way;
The name that can be named
Is not the constant name. Lao Tzu

All-inclusive, the Tao is a basic interrelating principle. From the Taoist point of view there is an essential unity between man and the various forces of nature.

In the Chinese tradition these forces are threefold: heaven, man, and earth. An ideogram expressing the relationship of "Heaven-Man-Earth" emphasizing the integral unity of these phenomena in a simple Mandala is:

Contained in this symbol is the realization that man is the center of the Mandala of the relationship between the heavenly and earthly forces. He is not considered apart, but as the composite of and intermediary between these energies. As an agent of the divine, man is able to transform the earthly powers. This capacity confers upon him a responsibility no longer generally recognized. Having denied the notion of inherent divinity, modern man has blinded himself to the upper line of the symbol; and, finding himself 'alone,' has considered himself the chief of the earth and all creation. But in the insecurity caused by denying what is essentially his own divinity, man has misused his powers to 'conquer' the earth. This is an unnecessary act according to the meaning of the symbol, since he is by *by nature* in a harmonious relationship with what is above—heaven—and what is below—earth. Man is the resonating agent who transforms the energies of above—of the psychic realms, and of the mind—into the energies of below—of matter, the sense-body, and the things pertaining to the senses; and vice versa. This is also the psychophysical point of view: psychic energy is continually transformed into physical energy, and physical into psychic. Man becomes the meeting ground and instrument of active and passive energies. He is the conscious center of the Mandala which heaven and earth are in the process of creating.

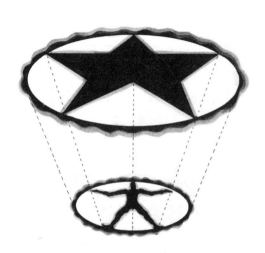

This triad symbol of Heaven-Man-Earth is suggestive of the basic component of the symbolic system of the *I Ching* or *Book of Changes.* The *pa kua* (or so called "trigrams") are constructed of three lines, one above the other. Each line symbolizes one of the three basic forces: the top line, heaven, and its alternations of light and dark; the bottom line, earth, in its aspects of yielding and firm; and the middle line, man, in his qualities of love and rectitude. These three lines are either solid __ or broken _ _, representing respectively the *yang*—the heavenly, positive, male forces, and the *yin*—the earthly, negative, female forces. The two qualities may be seen as the light (*yang*) and dark (*yin*) forces of the universe. However, it would be a mistake to think that this idea implies a dualism, nor should it be taken as an invitation to become caught in the polarities. Everything in nature is a blend of these two forces. What is demanded is a holistic point of view so that an over-identification with either one of the terms is avoided. The light implies the dark, the male, the female—there is no absolute separation, for both create the whole. Herein lies some of the meaning behind the *t'ai chi* symbol. Within the whole which they comprise, the alternation of these two forces create the processes of nature and the entire universe, visible and invisible.

In the *Book of Changes,* this simple principle of alternating bipolar rhythms —*change*—is developed into a unique and complex cosmology, philosophy, psychology, and divinatory text. To describe the multifarious processes implied by such an all-embracing system, the eight basic symbols of change—the *pa kua*—are doubled and placed one on top of the other to form a six line structure, the *kua* (or so-called "hexagram"). The combinations of this process yield sixty-four *kua* which symbolize the various stages of change common to all phenomena.

Despite this complexity, knowledge of the system of changes is based upon the *pa kua*—their growth from the primordial void, *wu chi*, and their developing interrelationships. From ancient times to the present, two arrangements of the *pa kua* in Mandala form have been transmitted: The Mandala of the Earlier Heaven, or Primal Arrangement; and the Mandala of the Later Heaven, or Inner World Arrangement (see next page).

In the Primal Arrangement the eight fundamental force symbols of the universe are grouped as four sets of polarities reflecting and complementing each other in a principle of inverse symmetry. Since the opposing forces are mutually inverse, and inversion is a basic law of harmony, the forces complement each other, and held together by the eternal center, the sum total comprises the archetypal atom of an ordered universe. The dynamism of complementary inversion precludes the stasis of polarization. It has been said: "He who can master the Sequence of Earlier Heaven, or Primal Arrangement, no longer has need of the Book of Changes."

> Heaven and earth determine the direction
> The forces of Mountain and Lake are united.
> Thunder and Wind arouse each other.
> Water and Fire do not combat each other.
> Thus are the eight pa kua intermingled.
>
> "Shuo Kua" I Ching

As its name implies, the Later Heaven or Inner World Arrangement exemplifies the cyclically interactive flow of the archetypal forces of change as they relate to the creation of the phenomenal world, and even more significantly, to the world of our inner, psychological responses. Just as the day has its rhythm corresponding to the larger one of the year, so man has an inner rhythm that can be attuned to greater and lesser cycles. The Inner World Arrangement is a concentrative means of harmonizing the tumult of the psyche with the laws of nature. Some of the Taoist traditions relate the flow of *pa kua* in this arrangement to breathing and meditational exercises. Each day man is born and dies anew; each day has its manrise and manset; each man his sunrise and sunset.

Mandala of the Earlier Heaven, or Primal Arrangement

Mandala of the Later Heaven, or Inner World Arrangement.

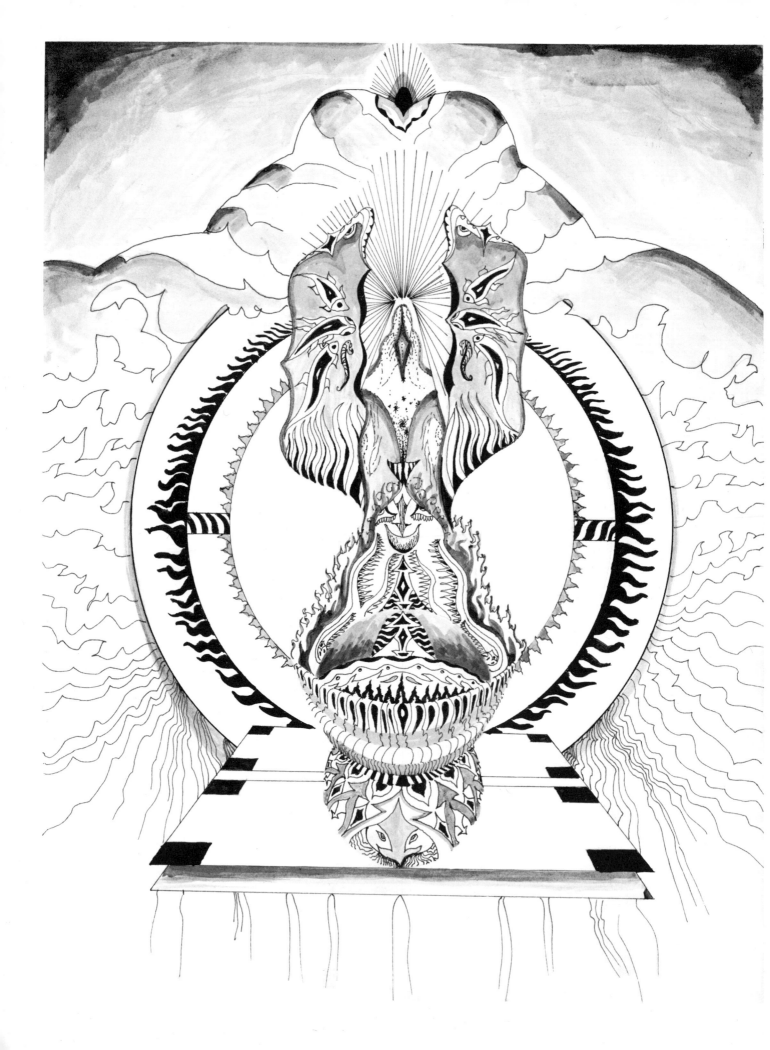

God comes forth in the sign of the Arousing;
He brings all things to completion in the sign of the Gentle;
He causes creatures to perceive each other in the sign of the Clinging (light);
He causes them to serve one another in the sign of the Receptive;
He gives them joy in the sign of the Joyous;
He battles in the sign of the Creative;
He toils in the sign of the Abysmal;
He brings them to perfection in the sign of Keeping Still.

"Shuo Kua", I Ching

All cycles of experience are interlinked and are the expression of one immutable law. The two arrangements of the *pa kua* complement each other: The Primal Arrangement manifests the essential harmony of the universe; the Inner World Arrangement, the rhythmic flow of this harmony phenomenally expressed. Wilhelm comments: "To understand fully, one must always visualize the Inner World Arrangement as transparent, with the Primal Arrangement shining through it."

The basic forces create and sustain each other through the mysterious power of the center. From this center flows the evolution of all phenomena in a symmetrically radiating manner. This is a cosmogenic process, which is beautifully described in the "Great Treatise" of the *Book of Changes:*

> *Therefore they called the closing of the gates the Receptive and the opening of the gates the Creative. The alternation between opening and closing they called change. The going forward and backward without ceasing they called penetration. What manifests visibly they called an image. What has bodily form they called a tool. What is established in usage they called a pattern. That which furthers on going out and coming in, that which all men live by they called the Divine.*

The reference to the "gates" pertains to the center, whose very existence evokes a polar movement—in and out—from which the various manifestations, visible and invisible, emanate in a concentric manner. The Mandala is not only a spatial axiom, but a temporal process as well. The Primal Arrangement of the *pa kua* also contains a forward and a backward motion. Concerning this dual movement, a commentary reads:

> *When the* pa kua *intermingle, that is, when they are in motion, a double movement is observable: first, the usual clockwise movement, cumulative and expanding as time goes on, and determining the events that are passing; second, an opposite, backward movement; folding up and contracting as time goes on, through which the seeds of the future take form. To know this movement is to know the future. In figurative terms, if we understand how a tree is contracted into a seed, we understand the future unfolding of the seed into a tree.*

Pervading and making this entire process possible is the divine principle "which all men live by." The fundamental principle of mystical thought and symbolism is *divine union,* which is not to be conceived of as a static, but as a dynamic process—if it is to be conceived of at all. This union is indivisible, it is the whole; *one* alone does not describe it. Divine Union is the central focus underlying things. Synergistically, it includes all the parts of the whole, but is not merely the sum. The dynamic wholeness which the Mandala comprises develops in accordance with very simple and general principles.

59

Everything the Power of
the World does is done in a circle. The
sky is round, and I have heard that the earth
is round like a ball, and so are all the stars. The wind,
in its greatest power, whirls. Birds make their nests in
circles, for theirs is the same religion as ours. The sun comes
forth and goes down again in a circle. The moon does the same,
and both are round. Even the seasons form a great circle in their
changing, and always come back again to where they were. The life
of a man is a circle from childhood to childhood, and so it is in everything where power moves. Our tepees were round like the nests of birds,
and these were always set in a circle, the nation's hoop, a nest of many
nests, where the Great Spirit meant for us to hatch our children.
Black Elk,
Black Elk Speaks

Laurette Séjourné speaks of the Law of the Center which "prevents the
splitting asunder of opposing forces." Cycles, whether pertaining to life and
death, space and time, visible and invisible forces, are held together in concentric patterns. Understanding the Law of the Center as a basic principle
of nature, men have been able to construct vast systems, and to perceive various
levels of order throughout the universe. From the Law of the Center, men
have also derived a developmental or even hierarchical ordering principle. Since
the center itself is identified with a source of power, wisdom and life, it occupies
the "highest" or innermost place within the entire concentric arrangement. The
center is the "nameless," the most supreme, the oldest, yet is ever-present and
continually pours forth its energy—it is self-renewing.

Abu Bakr Siraj Ed-Din speaks of this center principle as the Essence, and
compares it to a fire in which all is burnt, and also to a fountain—the Fountain
of Paradise—from which all pours forth. The realm of the Essence is the unitive

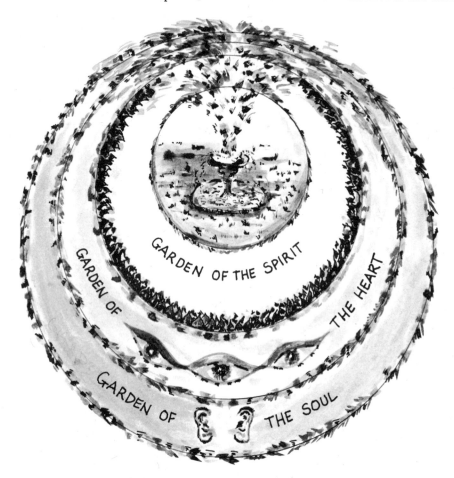

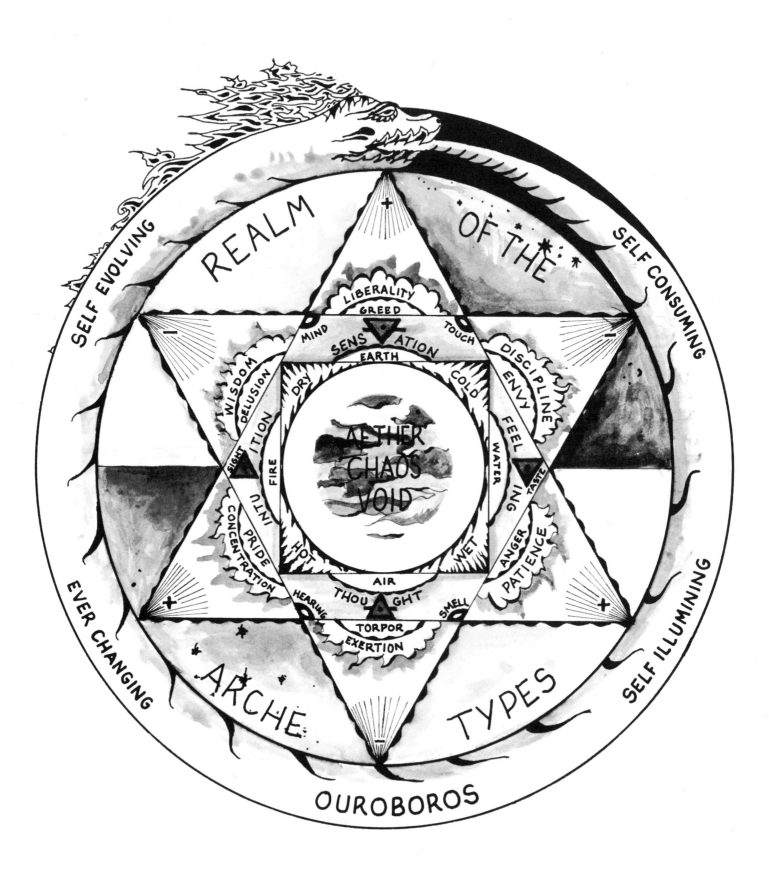

experience. Radiating outward from this Essence, and to be understood in a descending order, are various "lesser" realms of consciousness. In the imagery developed by the Muslim, Ed-Din, the closest realm to the central Garden of the Essence—which encompasses all the other Gardens—is the Garden of the Spirit; then comes the Garden of the Heart, and finally that of the Soul. The experience of the seeker at the center of this Mandala is the Certainty of the Essence. In this central experience, all things are burned away. In the Garden of the Spirit, the seeker knows the truth of Certainty, for he experiences the heat of the flame. In the Garden of the Heart, the seeker knows with the Eye of Certainty, for from this distance he can only see the flames of the Essence. In the Garden of the Soul, however, the seeker knows only from the Lore of Certainty, that is, from what he has been told.

Abu Bakr Siraj Ed-Din's description is a Mandala of manifold meaning. It describes the path of the seeker; it also implies a cosmogeny and a creative unfolding. Its hierarchical ordering is not to be thought of as a necessarily linear, sequential phenomenon. Instead, it is a Mandala operating at various levels simultaneously, much like a set of corresponding reflections in a series of pools, layered one upon the other, and all contained within one sea.

As a cosmogenic model, the Mandala is a synchronous, self-renewing whole. It has no beginning but the present moment, referred to in the Sufi traditions as the "Renewing of Creation at each instant." The idea of the essence of the Mandala as a process of continual renewal is close to that of *Heng*, "Duration," the thirty-second *kua* from the *Book of Changes:*

> *"Duration is a state whose movement is not worn down by hindrances. It is not a state of rest, for mere standstill is regression. Duration is rather the self-contained and therefore self-renewing movement of an organized, firmly integrated whole, taking place in accordance with immutable laws and beginning anew at every ending. The end is reached by an inward movement, by inhalation, systole, contraction, and this movement turns into a new beginning, in which the movement is directed outward, in exhalation, diastole, expansion.*
>
> *Heavenly bodies exemplify duration. They move in their fixed orbits, and because of this their light-giving power endures. The seasons of the year follow a fixed law of change and transformation, hence can produce effects that endure."*

The Emerald Table of Hermes Trismegistus.

Ongoing awareness of and participation in this creative self-renewing constitutes a fundamental alchemical activity. Alchemy is the conscious transmutation of one element into another, by whatever technique. Through words the poet transmutes feelings into song; through his love the lover transmutes the beloved into a being whose only rapture is to be extinguished in the love of the lover.

In its very psychophysical processes the human organism is continually alchemizing—transforming sense-data into psychic perception, and vice versa. Because of its transmutative and multi-dimensional nature, it is not surprising that much of what is called the alchemical tradition of the East and West has been transmitted through symbols, such as the Mandala or Magic Circle. Many of the leading practitioners of alchemy have been, for all intents and purposes, Symbolists.

Because alchemy has been transmitted through an intricate set of symbols which often refer to processes analogous to metallurgy, many a soul has been led astray. In the alchemical tradition a distinction is made between the true practitioners of the art—the Symbolists and Seekers—and the "charcoal burners"—those set on attaining a mere physical transmutation. If lead or gold are spoken of, it is understood that they refer as much to psychological qualities and processes, as to minerals from the earth. To the aspirant, the world is a ta-

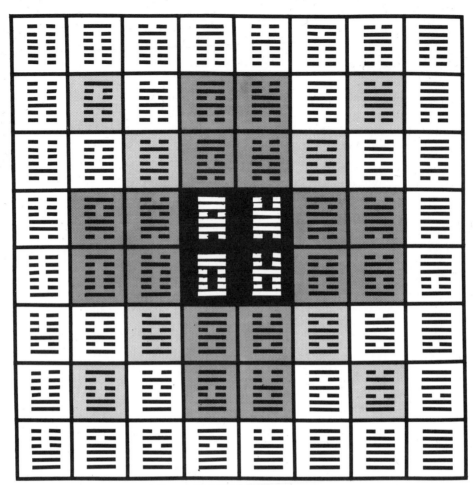

(Above) Mandala of Sixty-Four Kua.

(Below) Mandala of Sixty-Four Divisions, from the Vastu-Purusha-Mandala.

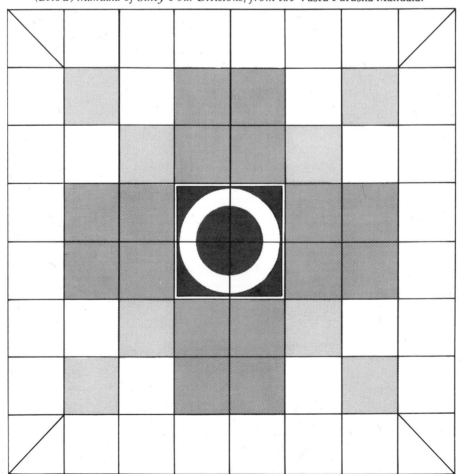

pestry of symbols, and the task is to perceive the correspondences so that he may achieve the Great Work: the transmutation of the soul.

The holistic perception of alchemy relates directly to the Mandala. Many alchemical charts take on a Mandala form in revealing the integral interrelationships between the elements and qualities of nature. Alchemy also defines the processes of consciousness as an on-going state of integral awareness, more precisely put by Dane Rudhyar as "interrelatedness in action."

As an alchemical technique, the *I Ching* furthers the active participation of man in the totality of the elements of which he is comprised, to which he contributes, and with which he consciously interacts in a mutually transformative process. The entirety of this dynamism describes nature: Heaven-Man-Earth—as an organic, evolutive whole.

To delineate this cosmic whole, the eight basic symbols of change—the *pa kua*—are expanded into a Mandala of that number squared: sixty-four. Building up from eight basic elements to sixty-four compounds is analogous to the alchemical process of multiplication. The Mandala of Sixty-Four *Kua* represents the structure of the cycle of changes comprising the most fundamental configurations of phenomena. The six line structure of each of these sixty-four symbols generally depicts the course of development of a given archetypal situation. From the point of view of the *Book of Changes,* all situations are archetypes or symbols which we construe (or misconstrue) according to the nature and development of our perceptions and consciousness. Since archetypes are what give form to the "collective unconscious," awareness of the archetypes in everyday living is a means by which the elements of existence may acquire a more conscious structure. Situations exist for the purpose of our being able to center and create ourselves anew through them.

Given the cyclically interrelated structure of the sixty-four symbols of the *I Ching*, it is significant that one of the basic visualization structures of the Hindu tradition is the Mandala of sixty-four divisions. This is one of the two basic Mandalas used in the plans of Indian temples, and is a member of the *Vastu-Purusha-Mandala,* a system of thirty-two types of Mandala formations. This system as a whole is broadly similar to the structural and permutational aspects of the *Book of Changes.*

The *Vastu-Purusha-Mandala* is the symbol of the unconditioned essence *(Purusha)* insofar as this essence is capable of lending itself to existence *(Vastu).* When the essence takes on existence it is given the form of a Mandala. This was considered by the ancient Hindus as being literally a *divine incorporation,* and the individual Mandalas as symbolic of the earth or earth principle. Originally, the *Vastu-Purusha-Mandala* corresponded to a live sacrifice symbolizing the beginning of a new world system. This ritual reflects the essence sacrificing its unconditioned beatitude, inaugurating existence in all its forms.

The thirty-two types of the *Vastu-Purusha-Mandala* are built up from groups of squares. There is a fundamental Mandala built up of nine squares, a symbol of the terrestial realm, with the central square corresponding to the center of the world. This is the central core of all the odd numbered Mandalas.

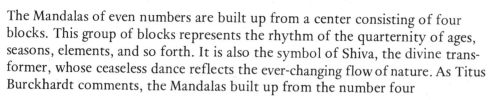

The Mandalas of even numbers are built up from a center consisting of four blocks. This group of blocks represents the rhythm of the quarternity of ages, seasons, elements, and so forth. It is also the symbol of Shiva, the divine transformer, whose ceaseless dance reflects the ever-changing flow of nature. As Titus Burckhardt comments, the Mandalas built up from the number four

> "... may be looked upon as the 'static' form of the cosmic wheel with four spokes, or divided into its four phases. It will be observed that this type of Mandala has no central square, the 'center' of time being the eternal present."

The same cyclo-cosmic and synchronistic principles govern both the *Book of Changes* and the *Vastu-Purusha-Mandala* of sixty-four divisions. The four central blocks representing Shiva correspond to the four central symbols of the *I Ching* Mandala of Sixty-Four *Kua*. These symbols: *Sun,* the "Penetrating" ䷸ ; *Heng,* "Duration" ䷟ ; *I,* "Increase" ䷩ ; and *Chen,* the "Arousing" ䷲ are comprised of the two *pa kua* the "Penetrating," Wind ☴ , and the "Arousing," Thunder ☳ . Together, Wind and Thunder form the active, transformative principles as they are manifest in the world of natural phenomena. In the psychic realm, their mutual interactivity is complementary: through the penetration of insight, dormant functions are aroused and made active.

> *Thunder rolls, and the wind blows; both are examples of extreme mobility and so are seemingly the very opposite of duration, but the the laws governing their appearance and subsidence, their coming and going, endure. In the same way the independence of the superior man is not based on rigidity and immobility of character. He always keeps abreast of the time and changes with it. What endures is the unswerving directive, the inner law of his being, which determines all his actions.*
>
> "Duration," *I Ching*

The amazingly fluid capacity for transformation also describes the law upon which Shiva's dance is based—the dance of the continual turning of the four-spoked cosmic wheel whose hub is eternity, and which transforms everything as it gradually rolls along its course.

The principle of Duration is synonomous with the dynamic principle of the Mandala. The Mandala is a cosmic diagram coordinating the cycles of space and time, uniting the way of heaven with the way of earth. The Mandala is often associated with the divine intelligence issuing from the supreme *Purusha.* And what this divine intelligence constructs through the process of Duration in the crystalline form of the sixty-four square Mandala is the structure of the City of God.

Sacred structures based on the Mandala are reflections of the cyclo-cosmic functions of nature. The sixty-four square Mandala has a border of twenty-eight squares. One obvious correspondence is with the lunar cycle of twenty-eight days, and in the Hindu astrological tradition, the twenty-eight lunar mansions. Similarly, the circular Sioux Indian ceremonial Sun Lodge is built with twenty-eight poles. The lodge itself becomes a cosmic symbol, representing the marriage of the sun—the lodge as a whole—and the moon—the structure of the lodge. In addition to the twenty-eight poles, there is an all-sustaining ridge pole at the center. Often this is a tree, symbolizing the axis of the world. The Sioux holy men say that this pole or tree represents Wakan Tanka, the spirit which sustains the universe.

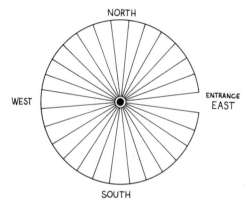

Sun Lodge.

In the Kabalistic tradition, twenty-eight is the number of the whole man, who is conceived as the sum of the triune aspects of spirit, soul, and body. Twenty-eight is the sum of 1+2+3+4+5+6+7 which can be represented by a triangle with one at the apex and seven at the base. Three cycles of twenty-eight years—eighty-four—are accordingly the ideal length of a human lifetime.

As a system which deals with the nature and influence of cyclo-cosmic rhythms, astrology is also characterized by the use of Mandalas. The symbols of the zodiac, commonly thought of as being solely celestial in nature, describe various psychological and terrestial processes. In recent times, Dane Rudhyar has most eloquently perceived the integral function of astrology and its relation to the Mandala:

> *The great symbol of individuation is the mandala: that is, a magic circle containing a cross or some other basically fourfold formulation.*
>
> *Such a symbol is the zodiac—and the typical quadrature of an astrological chart (the four angles). All natal astrology is the practical application of the 'squaring of the circle'—the conscious Way: Tao. Fourfold T-A-O gives the twelve signs of the houses of astrology (3x4=12). Every birth chart is the mandala of an individual life. It is the blueprint of the process of individuation for this particular individual. To follow it understandingly is to follow the 'conscious way;' the way of 'operative wholeness;' that is, the way of the active fulfillment of the wholeness of being that is Self.*

Each of the twelve zodiacal signs is associated with an elemental symbol— earth: Taurus, Virgo, and Capricorn; air: Gemini, Libra, and Aquarius; fire: Aries, Leo, and Sagittarius; and water: Cancer, Scorpio, and Pisces. These signs correspond to the quarternary flow of the seasons, and to a specific activity according to the following scheme:

At the Spring Equinox: *Fire-power is generated—Aries*
  then concentrated—Taurus
  lastly distributed—Gemini
At the Summer Solstice: *Water-power is generated—Cancer*
  then concentrated—Leo
  lastly distributed—Virgo
At the Fall Equinox: *Air-power is generated—Libra*
  then concentrated—Scorpio
  lastly distributed—Sagittarius
At the Winter Solstice: *Earth-power is generated—Capricorn*
  then concentrated—Aquarius
  lastly distributed—Pisces

Zodiacal signs of generative power are called cardinal signs.
Zodiacal signs of concentration of power are called fixed signs.
Zodiacal signs of distribution of power are called mutable signs.

This cycle of symbols describes activities which are universally operative and, when applied to man, create the possibility of the "Zodiac as the Cycle of the Planetary Individual." The individual mandalized as the zodiac is a symbol of the fulfillment of universal selfhood. Identified in this way the individual is capable of participating in a process of what Rudhyar calls "organic living— which always involves three basic faculties: self-maintenance, self-reproduction, self-realization." These may be related respectively to the concentrative, generative and distributive qualities of the zodiacal signs.

Organic living itself is based on a harmonization with, and a direct actualization of an all-sustaining power or set of energies. Harmonically actualized, the individual organism becomes a field of energy. The energy of this field operates on a fundamentally polar rhythm of positive + and negative -, or, in the language of the *I Ching*, in solid —— and broken – –, *yang* and *yin*, lines.

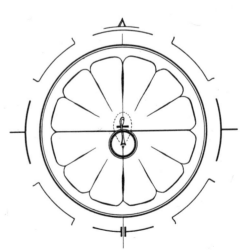

Astrological Chart.

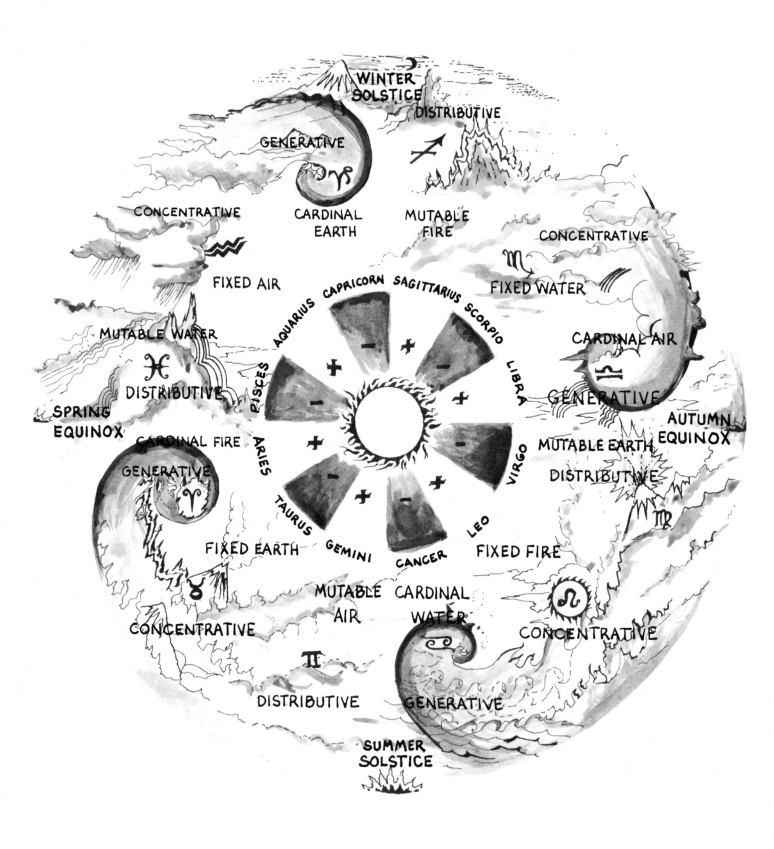

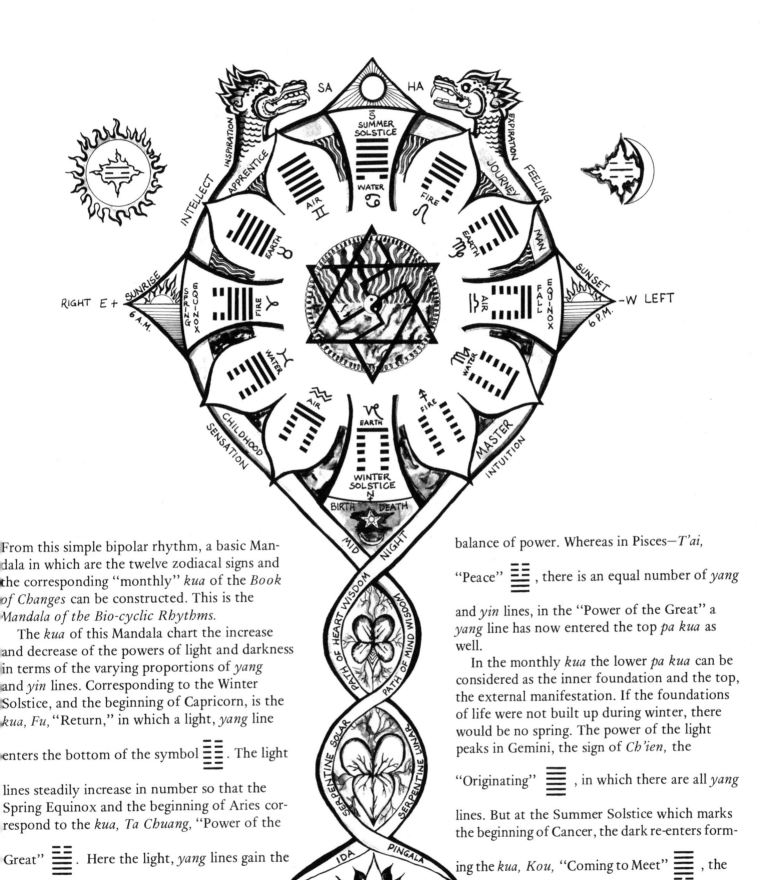

From this simple bipolar rhythm, a basic Mandala in which are the twelve zodiacal signs and the corresponding "monthly" *kua* of the *Book of Changes* can be constructed. This is the *Mandala of the Bio-cyclic Rhythms.*

The *kua* of this Mandala chart the increase and decrease of the powers of light and darkness in terms of the varying proportions of *yang* and *yin* lines. Corresponding to the Winter Solstice, and the beginning of Capricorn, is the *kua, Fu,* "Return," in which a light, *yang* line

enters the bottom of the symbol. The light

lines steadily increase in number so that the Spring Equinox and the beginning of Aries correspond to the *kua, Ta Chuang,* "Power of the

Great". Here the light, *yang* lines gain the

balance of power. Whereas in Pisces—*T'ai,*

"Peace", there is an equal number of *yang*

and *yin* lines, in the "Power of the Great" a *yang* line has now entered the top *pa kua* as well.

In the monthly *kua* the lower *pa kua* can be considered as the inner foundation and the top, the external manifestation. If the foundations of life were not built up during winter, there would be no spring. The power of the light peaks in Gemini, the sign of *Ch'ien,* the

"Originating", in which there are all *yang*

lines. But at the Summer Solstice which marks the beginning of Cancer, the dark re-enters forming the *kua, Kou,* "Coming to Meet", the

Mandala of Bio-cyclic Rhythms.

inverse of "Return." The dark begins at the peak of the power of the light, and the light returns in the dark of night. Though the summer is externally manifest as light and power, its foundation, symbolized by the lower *pa kua* is increasingly absorbed by the *yin* powers. The Fall Equinox is represented by the *kua,*

Kuan, "Contemplation" 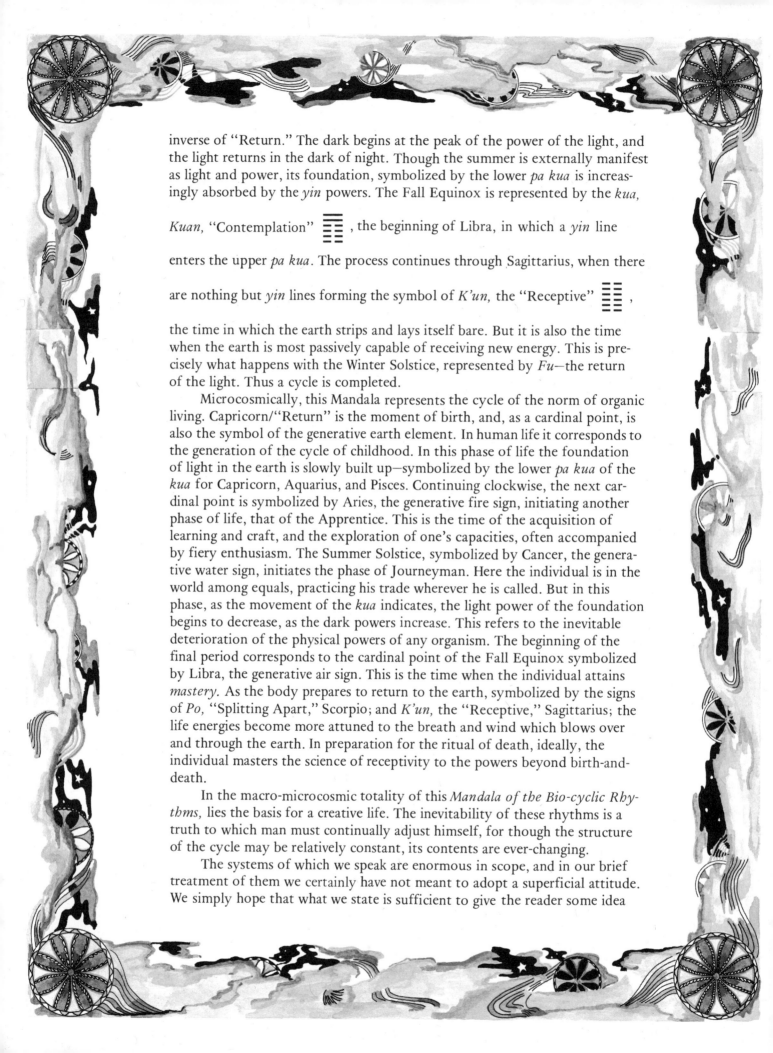, the beginning of Libra, in which a *yin* line

enters the upper *pa kua*. The process continues through Sagittarius, when there

are nothing but *yin* lines forming the symbol of *K'un,* the "Receptive" ,

the time in which the earth strips and lays itself bare. But it is also the time when the earth is most passively capable of receiving new energy. This is precisely what happens with the Winter Solstice, represented by *Fu*—the return of the light. Thus a cycle is completed.

Microcosmically, this Mandala represents the cycle of the norm of organic living. Capricorn/"Return" is the moment of birth, and, as a cardinal point, is also the symbol of the generative earth element. In human life it corresponds to the generation of the cycle of childhood. In this phase of life the foundation of light in the earth is slowly built up—symbolized by the lower *pa kua* of the *kua* for Capricorn, Aquarius, and Pisces. Continuing clockwise, the next cardinal point is symbolized by Aries, the generative fire sign, initiating another phase of life, that of the Apprentice. This is the time of the acquisition of learning and craft, and the exploration of one's capacities, often accompanied by fiery enthusiasm. The Summer Solstice, symbolized by Cancer, the generative water sign, initiates the phase of Journeyman. Here the individual is in the world among equals, practicing his trade wherever he is called. But in this phase, as the movement of the *kua* indicates, the light power of the foundation begins to decrease, as the dark powers increase. This refers to the inevitable deterioration of the physical powers of any organism. The beginning of the final period corresponds to the cardinal point of the Fall Equinox symbolized by Libra, the generative air sign. This is the time when the individual attains *mastery.* As the body prepares to return to the earth, symbolized by the signs of *Po,* "Splitting Apart," Scorpio; and *K'un,* the "Receptive," Sagittarius; the life energies become more attuned to the breath and wind which blows over and through the earth. In preparation for the ritual of death, ideally, the individual masters the science of receptivity to the powers beyond birth-and-death.

In the macro-microcosmic totality of this *Mandala of the Bio-cyclic Rhythms,* lies the basis for a creative life. The inevitability of these rhythms is a truth to which man must continually adjust himself, for though the structure of the cycle may be relatively constant, its contents are ever-changing.

The systems of which we speak are enormous in scope, and in our brief treatment of them we certainly have not meant to adopt a superficial attitude. We simply hope that what we state is sufficient to give the reader some idea

Mercy - Choice.

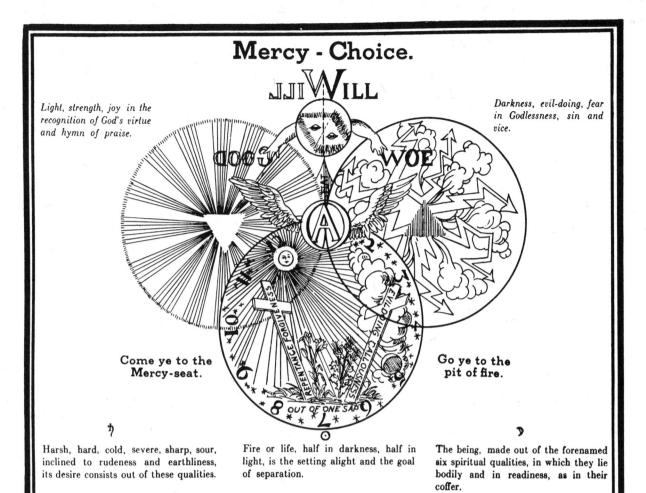

Light, strength, joy in the recognition of God's virtue and hymn of praise.

Darkness, evil-doing, fear in Godlessness, sin and vice.

Come ye to the Mercy-seat.

Go ye to the pit of fire.

♄

Harsh, hard, cold, severe, sharp, sour, inclined to rudeness and earthliness, its desire consists out of these qualities.

Fire or life, half in darkness, half in light, is the setting alight and the goal of separation.

☽

The being, made out of the forenamed six spiritual qualities, in which they lie bodily and in readiness, as in their coffer.

☿

Fear, heat, therein consist the Bitter, drawing and moving out of the harsh quality, which causes a sting within, and remains in that spirit, the existence of mobility.

♂

The first and dark Principium. God the Father, being called a consuming fire.

The other Principium of light, being God's Son, is one with the eternal world of light.

✶

Is the power from the life of Light, love, fire, which burns light, in it is fulfilled God's word of the cognition, sound, consists the heavenly life.

♀

in the oil of Mercy, in which call and tone.

The Principium of the fire belongs to the world of the four elements, being an offspring of the first two, and is the third principle.

Whenever the first three qualities of the first dark Principii gain the upper hand, then the others are tied up around their Centro and all seven are evil. Then Saturnus stands for avarice, Mercurius for envy, Mars for wrath, Sol for vanity, Venus for lewdness, Jupiter for cunning and Luna for bodily desire, which are the seven evil spirits ruling within the old human being.

But when the three in the Principio of light have the upper-hand and are born out of the dark Centro, so that they are in accordance with their innermost depths of light, which is the new birth in man, all seven are good, and then Saturnus stands for compassion, Mercurius for doing good, Mars for gentleness, Sol for humility, Venus for chastity, Jupiter for wisdom, and Luna for Christ's flesh or body.

of the universal adaptiveness of the Mandala principle and of its appropriateness in being applied to an understanding of symbolic systems.

The Mandala is a metaphysical structuring principle. Symbolic systems are valid for human development to the degree that they point to a way of creative living—the conscious attunement of man to the cosmic rhythms so that his daily life manifests in every way a sense of harmony.

An arrangement of symbols alone does not necessarily create a Mandala or a way of consciousness. Unless a more inclusive and integrative principle is implied, an arrangement—no matter how mathematically perfect—is without life. The ancient adepts of alchemy practiced what we might today call science. But theirs was a science of *orientation*—which literally means facing the Orient, the East, where the sun rises. Orientation has a further meaning which implies being based on a knowledge of the cosmic coordinates, that is, *of the whole.* Holistic knowledge operates on what Einstein described as a unified field theory—a formula, or integrating principle by which all of the different processes and functions of the universe are related. Such a formula would also bring together the different bodies and techniques subsumed under the broad name of science. Art and religion, because they, too, are ways of knowing, would then be integrally bound to what is now more narrowly defined as science; and these three would be one gnostic whole.

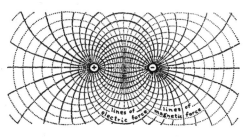

Field diagram.

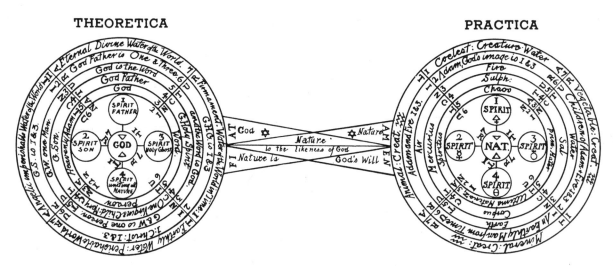

In such a knowledge system there is no separation between theory and practice. Its very foundation is awe and reverence toward the creative forces of the universe. When man ceases to revere nature, his knowledge of nature also ceases to be fully integrated into his way of life. When this process begins, no matter how precise man's knowledge may be, it tends to have less relevance to the laws and practice of life, and may even become destructive of life. Rather than leading him to a greater harmony with nature, man's precise but fragmented and fragmenting sciences lead him into a state of dissonance. One prominent cosmologist, Oliver Reiser, states the present-day situation clearly: "The scientists have not integrated the bodies of knowledge (sciences) into a unified interpretation of man, his place in nature and his potentialities for creating the good society."

Man has the potential to become more fully conscious and coordinate his efforts to re-establish or actually re-harmonize the foundations of his knowledge, so that it may lead him once again on a harmonic way. What is meant by harmony or a harmonic way is not only an *at-one-ness* of the elements of nature, but also a *resonance* of these elements. When man harmonizes he consciously resonates or attunes himself to the various energies of nature and to the cycles which these energies create. As modern physics has reconfirmed, there is nothing but energy and on-going energy fields which are developed, take form and function according to specific laws. These laws, however formulated, are univer-

Plate 6: *Game of Spheres.* Roberto Matiello.

Plate 7: *Four Houses of the Sun.* David Villaseñor, *Tapestries in Sand.*

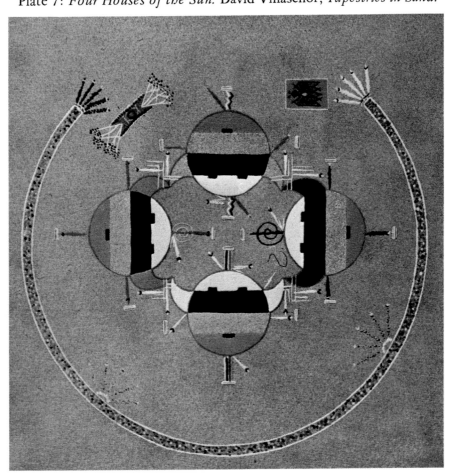

Plate 8:
Mahakala.
Courtesy of
Samuel
Bercholz.

Plate 9:
Wheel of Life.
Courtesy of
Jack Weller.

Plate 10: *Mandala of Samvara.* Tibetan Tanka. Courtesy of the
Center of Asian Art and Culture, The Avery Brundage Collection, San Francisco, California.

sal and govern the coming into being, growth, decay, and subsidence of all phenomena. The energy field of man is no exception.

The theory of man as an on-going resonant energy field is by no means a new one. In man, this field constitutes visible, dense physical organs—brain, and nervous systems, vital organs, glands and the sense body itself—as well as invisible or etheric organs. According to resonant field theory, there are various vibrating forces or etheric centers in which different levels of energy are concentrated or focalized, and which create an etheric body corresponding to, interwoven with, and encompassing the dense physical body. In the Christian tradition the halo and aureole—hence aura—refer to this etheric body. The whole of the dense and etheric bodies may be described in modern terms as a bio-psychic energy spectrum.

The form of this radiant energy spectrum is spherical, a vibratory, pulsating Mandala, with various centers, each emanating a qualitative energy field. When fully developed, these individual centers and their fields create the full bio-psychic spectrum. In many Eastern and Western occult systems the etheric centers are referred to as the Chakras. (See Plate 13.) Chakra literally means "circle" or "wheel"; it is often visualized as a lotus Mandala. The science of the Chakras constitutes yet another symbolic system. A very definite set of correspondences exists between these mutually inclusive and complementary systems: they are but individual fibers woven into One.

The number of Chakras varies according to the specific tradition. The Hopi Indians recognize at least five etheric centers. These include the "door" at the top of the head, where the energy enters the body, as well as four lower centers corresponding to the brain or mind center; the throat, or center of speech, breath, and sound; the heart, the basic life center; and the solar plexus, otherwise known as the *throne of the Creator.*

In the Hindu tradition there are two additional centers beneath the solar plexus—the *Svadhisthana,* related to the sexual functions, and the *Muladhara,* located in the area of the tip of the spine. The *Muladhara* is also recognized as the center of the basic life energy, or *Kundalini*—serpent power. In contrast to the Hopis, the Hindu Tantra system of Chakras emphasizes the necessity of raising energy from the lowest center to the highest, the *Sahasrara,* or "thousand petalled lotus" at the top of the skull. In the Hindu system, the first five Chakras (from the bottom up) are envisioned as beads strung on a thread known as the *chitra nadi* and are contained within the *susumna.* The *susumna,* an etheric axis, parallels the spinal axis. Upon leaving the sixth Chakra—the *Ajña*—the *susumna* culminates in the *Sahasrara.* Ascending up this column, each succeeding Chakra becomes associated with ever more refined and subtle functions, forms of energy, and planes of being. The etheric centers are also closely related to the various systems of glands, vital organs and nerve centers of the physical body.

Although the Tibetan system of the Chakras is developed from the Hindu in its terminology, general philosophical approach, and location of the centers, it has interesting points of similarity with the Hopi system: both systems recognize five centers and emphasize a *descent* of energy through the top of the head. On the other hand, it should be pointed out that the Tibetan tradition combines the two top and the two bottom Chakras recognized in Hindu Tantra, whereas the Hopi centers generally correspond to the top five of the Hindu tradition.

Western occult traditions recognize the seven Chakras described in the Hindu system. The Rosicrucians and Theosophists do not necessarily place these centers on a spinal axis, but rather, closer to the nerve centers of the physical organism to which the Chakras are related, i.e., spleen, solar plexus, heart, thyroid and pituitary glands. By contrast, the Chinese system is quite complex and is based on a circulatory movement from the top of the head

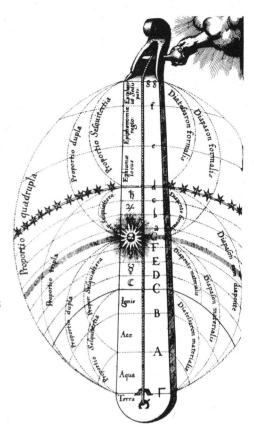

The Divine Monochord.

73

SOUTHERN CIRCUMPOLAR MAP
for each Month in the Year.

to the tip of the spine—the Mortal Gate—and back up again. Some of the basic centers are the Stove, located in the lower abdominal region; the House of Fire, or the heart; and the Precious Cauldron, located toward the top of the head. In the systems which we have mentioned a wealth of colors, sounds, functions, elements, and symbols, is associated with each of the centers.

What is significant about the Chakra system is that, like astrology or the *Book of Changes,* it presents a view of man as the microcosm. The axis of man—physical and etheric—is analogous to the axis of the world. The etheric column of this axis may be visualized as the center of a resonant energy field Mandala. The energy sources along this axis are the Chakras, each pulsing and sending out a vortex field of a specific quality of energy. These vortices, however many in number, when fully activated function according to the hierarchical structuring principle of resonance. That is, when each succeeding center is activated, its vibrational tone includes the tones of all the centers below it and upon which it is based. But as in music, each tone has its overtones, and so it may also be said that the lowest contains the highest.

There is a universal recognition of psychic centers and a corresponding etheric body. Within the different systems, the number and functions of these centers, as well as the theories and practices regarding the activation and directional flow of energy through the centers, varies considerably. In specific cultural and geographical situations different energies are recognized for appropriate human development.

The general planetary significance of the recognition of the Chakras as an innate characteristic of the species is that it provides a base for a universal system of human harmonics. The energy which is harmonized corresponds to a field in which the human body is contained, much as the contents of the embryo are contained within the placenta. This is the auric field, or field of consciousness. Accordingly, man in his present state is potentially ready to activate this field, but the energies necessary for this activation lie dormant, or, at best, are only randomly and haphazardly aroused, and then very often to the detriment of the organism. When the Chakras are consciously activated, the individual becomes the center of a dynamic, on-going, self-integrated Mandala.

The idea of man's harmonization through the activation of the psychic energy centers represents a radical departure from most present theories and practices regarding the human organism. Implicit in a system of human harmonics is the notion that man himself is the greatest source of the energy he needs—not only to maintain, but also to heal and regenerate himself. Or, referring back to the definition of "organic living," the wholeness of man involves the interrelated activity of the three basic faculties: self-maintenance, self-reproduction, and self-realization.

In this vision of man, the Chakras are a system of biopsychic resonators. Attunement through these resonators may be the means by which man creates a more efficient and direct liaison with the creative forces of the cosmos. Were men to pursue ideas such as these, no doubt a base for a new unifying system of knowledge and science could be created, a system which would be to present-day science as present-day science is to the techniques operating at the tribal stage of human development. Man is a transition, an agent of transformation as well as the material to be transformed. This transformative operation can occur only through the focusing power of some new symbol or image of the whole process in which man now finds himself involved. In its universality, the Mandala provides at least the base structure for such a symbol.

Understanding the primordial symbolism of the Mandala can lead not only to greater awareness, but ultimately to a transformation of the very ways in which a man responds to the world in all its impulses. This is the alchemy of symbols whose source is the power residing in the Mandala, the Mother of Symbols. As the matrix of symbolic systems, the Mandala provides only the metaphysics of the ritual: the transmutation into spiritual man. What remains is the act itself, the rite without which there can be no new knowledge.

Man is a symbol. So is an object or a drawing. Penetrate beneath the outward message of the symbol or you will put yourself to sleep. . . Within the symbol there is a design which moves. Get to know this design. In order to do this you need a guide. But before he can help you, you must be prepared by exercising honesty towards the object of your search. If you seek truth and knowledge, you will gain it. If you seek something for yourself alone, you may gain it and lose all higher possibilities for yourself.

Kwaja Pulad of Erivan

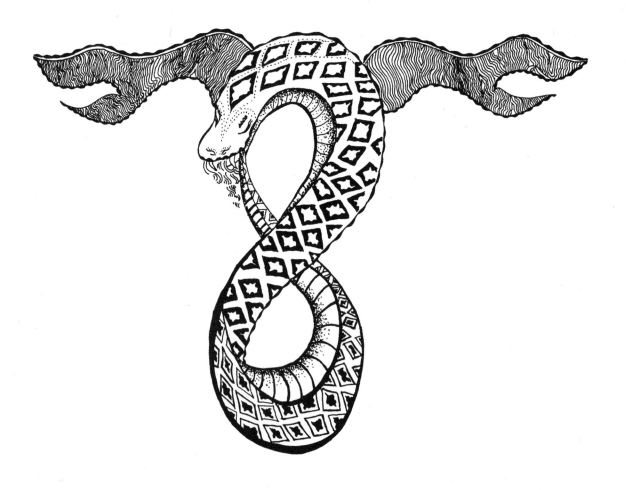

I am
the center
I am
the point
from which each direction goes
I am
the seed
from which time grows
and flows around me
In days that are without number
a thousand suns surround me
And I am the sun
burning in the center
I am
my rays go out
and penetrate the night
I am
a million jewels blazing
in my solar sight

I am
the past and future joined
set in eternal flight
I am
the morning and the evening
In my eternal light
I am
And yet in me
the silent mystery
"I am not"
forever burns
and I bow down
A silent witness
to what in me

forever learns
forever burns
forever turns

Notes

The *I Ching* is a fundamental aid in articulating the depth and scope of the Mandala as a key to symbolic systems. This is especially true of the contents of Book II in the Wilhelm/Baynes edition of the *I Ching* (Princeton: Princeton University Press, 1967), pp.255-365, which includes the "*Shuo Kua* or Discussion of the *[pa kua]* Trigrams," and the "*Ta Chuan* or Great Treatise," in which the principles and foundations of the *Book of Changes* are discussed and revealed. A technical point of clarification is our use of the Chinese terms *pa kua* for "trigram," and *kua* for "hexagrams." As Dr. Khiegh Dhiegh of the International I Ching Studies Institute (Los Angeles) has pointed out, to call the basic symbols of the *I Ching* "trigrams" and "hexagrams" is erroneous and misleading since the suffix "-gram" means a geometric figure of lines which touch or cross, whereas the lines of the *kua* are parallel. *Kua* literally means "line" or "sign"; *pa* means eight. Additional texts dealing with Chinese symbolic systems are the already cited *Tao Teh Ching* by Lao Tzu; and Lu K'uan Yu's *Taoist Yoga: Alchemy and Immortality.* By far the best sourcebook in this area is Fung Yu Lan, *A History of Chinese Philosophy* (Princeton: Princeton University Press, 1953).

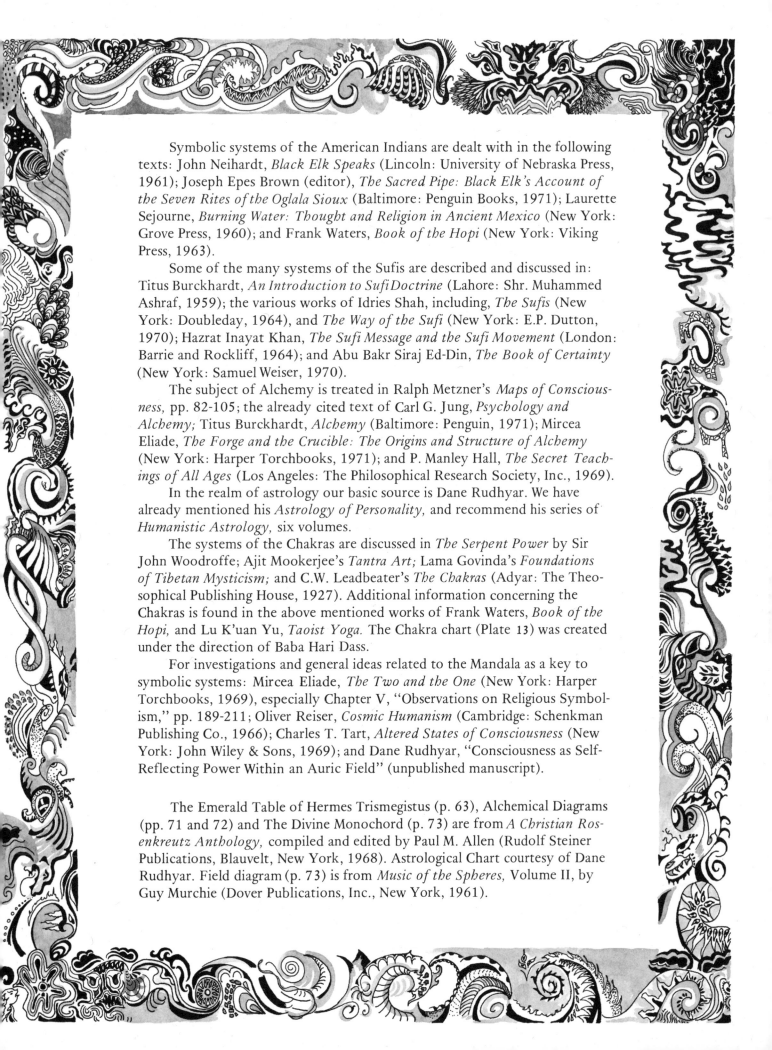

Symbolic systems of the American Indians are dealt with in the following texts: John Neihardt, *Black Elk Speaks* (Lincoln: University of Nebraska Press, 1961); Joseph Epes Brown (editor), *The Sacred Pipe: Black Elk's Account of the Seven Rites of the Oglala Sioux* (Baltimore: Penguin Books, 1971); Laurette Sejourne, *Burning Water: Thought and Religion in Ancient Mexico* (New York: Grove Press, 1960); and Frank Waters, *Book of the Hopi* (New York: Viking Press, 1963).

Some of the many systems of the Sufis are described and discussed in: Titus Burckhardt, *An Introduction to Sufi Doctrine* (Lahore: Shr. Muhammed Ashraf, 1959); the various works of Idries Shah, including, *The Sufis* (New York: Doubleday, 1964), and *The Way of the Sufi* (New York: E.P. Dutton, 1970); Hazrat Inayat Khan, *The Sufi Message and the Sufi Movement* (London: Barrie and Rockliff, 1964); and Abu Bakr Siraj Ed-Din, *The Book of Certainty* (New York: Samuel Weiser, 1970).

The subject of Alchemy is treated in Ralph Metzner's *Maps of Consciousness,* pp. 82-105; the already cited text of Carl G. Jung, *Psychology and Alchemy;* Titus Burckhardt, *Alchemy* (Baltimore: Penguin, 1971); Mircea Eliade, *The Forge and the Crucible: The Origins and Structure of Alchemy* (New York: Harper Torchbooks, 1971); and P. Manley Hall, *The Secret Teachings of All Ages* (Los Angeles: The Philosophical Research Society, Inc., 1969).

In the realm of astrology our basic source is Dane Rudhyar. We have already mentioned his *Astrology of Personality,* and recommend his series of *Humanistic Astrology,* six volumes.

The systems of the Chakras are discussed in *The Serpent Power* by Sir John Woodroffe; Ajit Mookerjee's *Tantra Art;* Lama Govinda's *Foundations of Tibetan Mysticism;* and C.W. Leadbeater's *The Chakras* (Adyar: The Theosophical Publishing House, 1927). Additional information concerning the Chakras is found in the above mentioned works of Frank Waters, *Book of the Hopi,* and Lu K'uan Yu, *Taoist Yoga.* The Chakra chart (Plate 13) was created under the direction of Baba Hari Dass.

For investigations and general ideas related to the Mandala as a key to symbolic systems: Mircea Eliade, *The Two and the One* (New York: Harper Torchbooks, 1969), especially Chapter V, "Observations on Religious Symbolism," pp. 189-211; Oliver Reiser, *Cosmic Humanism* (Cambridge: Schenkman Publishing Co., 1966); Charles T. Tart, *Altered States of Consciousness* (New York: John Wiley & Sons, 1969); and Dane Rudhyar, "Consciousness as Self-Reflecting Power Within an Auric Field" (unpublished manuscript).

The Emerald Table of Hermes Trismegistus (p. 63), Alchemical Diagrams (pp. 71 and 72) and The Divine Monochord (p. 73) are from *A Christian Rosenkreutz Anthology,* compiled and edited by Paul M. Allen (Rudolf Steiner Publications, Blauvelt, New York, 1968). Astrological Chart courtesy of Dane Rudhyar. Field diagram (p. 73) is from *Music of the Spheres,* Volume II, by Guy Murchie (Dover Publications, Inc., New York, 1961).

To Become One As the Flower Wedded to the Sun

V
The Ritual of the Mandala

To Him Who is the Lord of the Center
The Diamond Weaver
The Invisible Father of the Sun
Who is seated on the Throne of the Archetypes
Teller of the Fables of the Celestial Night
Dreamer of the Visions of All Men
Teacher of the Twelve-fold Rites of the Sun
Keeper of the Book of Days
Seed of the Names of All Things
Seer of All Entrances and Partings
He Who sets in motion the Elements and Seasons
And Who places the Rainbow Border on all Creation...

You, O Nameless One, we invoke:
Enter our hearts and speak through us
Lend to us the Vision of Unity
Teach us the Science of the Whole
Make known to us once again the Rite of the Mandala

Hear us, O Lord of the Center
Keeper of the Radiant Law
In our silence may Your Voice ring clear

We are as Seeds:
Only You Who walk the Sky
Can show to us the Path
Our feet must follow in this Earth
Only You can heal and make us whole
Only through our submission to You
May we heal ourselves and become whole—

In this way may we be led once again on the Path of Beauty.

Man is changing and the world about him is continually changing him—whether it is his own, "man-made" world, or the natural forces and elements that underlie and permeate this world. No sooner is one construct of the world created in his mind than it is destroyed. Nature mocks and devours man's dreams. Or is it man who places himself and his ideas so unwittingly in continual jeopardy by some blind spot in his makeup? Meditating upon the transitory nature of things, the philosopher might conclude that is it hopeless to attempt to control nature. Free will means nothing if man does not understand the nature of what he faces, and what he faces is immeasurably more than himself. Commonsense would seem to dictate the sublime law of submission in view of the immense reality with which man must cope.

> Do not imagine, think, analyze, meditate, act;
> Keep the mind in its natural state.
> Tilopa

The awesomeness of nature is predicated upon order and subject to change. Attunement with the laws by which the forces of nature are ordered, rise and pass away may provide the significance which man is ever seeking for his life. Knowledge through attunement to the greater laws of nature is akin to "the Goal beyond all Theories."

> Subdue oneself and recover the ritual disposition.
> Confucius

Ritual is not just a matter of doing, but more fundamentally, of subduing. It can be considered as a psychic technology for the exploration and synthesis of being. Ritual knowledge is not necessarily additional and discursive, but rather transformative. It accompanies important bio-organic transitions such as birth, puberty, marriage or death, and causes a qualitative change within the organism. All living creatures experience these changes in one way or another—the very definition of life is moving from one transformation to another in a continuum. Through ritual man attains at a more highly integrated level of organicity, the same sureness of instinct manifest by the various creatures of the animal kingdom. In man ritual is rooted in the intuitional realm of vision —his deeper nature. It is applied at those junctures of life when the order of things must be clearly seen, and the splendor of the greater Light allowed to shine through the purified passages of being.

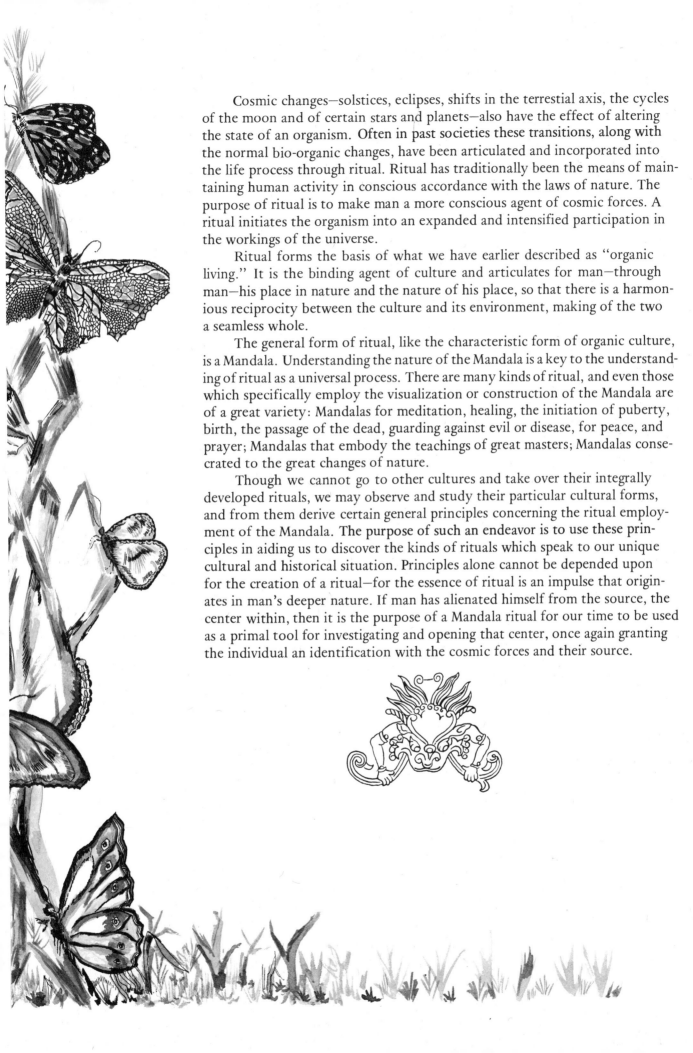

Cosmic changes—solstices, eclipses, shifts in the terrestial axis, the cycles of the moon and of certain stars and planets—also have the effect of altering the state of an organism. Often in past societies these transitions, along with the normal bio-organic changes, have been articulated and incorporated into the life process through ritual. Ritual has traditionally been the means of maintaining human activity in conscious accordance with the laws of nature. The purpose of ritual is to make man a more conscious agent of cosmic forces. A ritual initiates the organism into an expanded and intensified participation in the workings of the universe.

Ritual forms the basis of what we have earlier described as "organic living." It is the binding agent of culture and articulates for man—through man—his place in nature and the nature of his place, so that there is a harmonious reciprocity between the culture and its environment, making of the two a seamless whole.

The general form of ritual, like the characteristic form of organic culture, is a Mandala. Understanding the nature of the Mandala is a key to the understanding of ritual as a universal process. There are many kinds of ritual, and even those which specifically employ the visualization or construction of the Mandala are of a great variety: Mandalas for meditation, healing, the initiation of puberty, birth, the passage of the dead, guarding against evil or disease, for peace, and prayer; Mandalas that embody the teachings of great masters; Mandalas consecrated to the great changes of nature.

Though we cannot go to other cultures and take over their integrally developed rituals, we may observe and study their particular cultural forms, and from them derive certain general principles concerning the ritual employment of the Mandala. The purpose of such an endeavor is to use these principles in aiding us to discover the kinds of rituals which speak to our unique cultural and historical situation. Principles alone cannot be depended upon for the creation of a ritual—for the essence of ritual is an impulse that originates in man's deeper nature. If man has alienated himself from the source, the center within, then it is the purpose of a Mandala ritual for our time to be used as a primal tool for investigating and opening that center, once again granting the individual an identification with the cosmic forces and their source.

We wish to do two things: to give a description of the general principles of the ritual use of the Mandala, derived essentially from Tibetan and Navaho sources; and to present a few basic meditations, visualizations, and exercises for individual and group practice.

Principles

. . . a mandala delineates a consecrated place and protects it from invasion by disintegrating forces. . . But a mandala is much more than just a consecrated area that must be kept pure for ritual and liturgical ends. It is, above all, a map of the cosmos. It is the whole universe in its essential plan, in its process of emanation and of re-absorption. The universe not only in its inert spatial expanse, but as temporal revolution and both as a vital process which develops from an essential principle and rotates round a central axis, . . . the axis of the world on which the sky rests and which sinks its roots into the mysterious substratum.''

G. Tucci

This is the seed idea; the component parts of the process are:

Purification

Purification may take many forms and has many degrees of intensity. Of primary concern is the realization of its necessity. If the human organism is compared to a highly refined tuning and receiving set, purification may be regarded as a cleaning of the basic parts so that there is no static between internal organs blocking reception from afar. This often means a complete cleansing and purging of the body: at the very least, no intake of toxic elements, in some cases not even of solid food, or even liquids for a given period of time. Purificatory fasting initially gives an awareness of the body and of what we assume to be its demands; and secondly, because the consciousness is not clogged with the body's demands, it affords an opportunity to come to a more direct contact with the spiritual forces.

It is the tradition of the North American Indians, for instance, to fast for three or four days prior to an important event—including the creation of a sandpainting. As the Indians are aware, fasting of any prolonged form is extremely conducive to visions, and often accompanied by prayer. This is why purification is such a necessary aspect of the vision quest of the Native Americans. Purification has the further effect of stimulating the senses so that they will be more responsive during the ritual process.

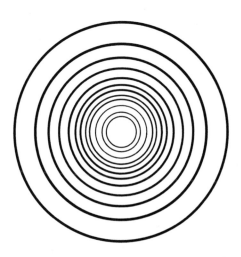

Centering

Closely related to the function of purifying the mind and body is centering or meditation. It is a con-centration—making con-centric—of the organism's outflowing energies by turning them inward and focusing them through a central point. In this way the biopsychic energies are literally recycled. Any activity which achieves this effect is a form of centering—this is often true of handicrafts: ceramics, carving, beadwork, weaving, and painting. The weaver's fingers and the potter's hands are moved by a vision emanating from the still point within, and the final craft is but a manifested form of the energies radiating from that still point to the mind, the eyes, and the fingers of the craftsman.

Be still, O my heart, be still and know God.

Often a seated position—either on a chair or in a variant of the lotus posture of the Yogis, is considered a necessary prerequisite for centering. It should be done in a quiet room or in a natural setting. The process of centering involves a slow dropping away of cares and concerns by trying to focus and hold the consciousness steady. Concentration devices are often introduced to help in the process. Such devices may include a silently repeated mantram:

OM MANI

PADME HUM

God I am one in Nature

Nature I am one in God

Visual concentrative images may be a simple sun or flower depicted in the mind's eye, or a more complex linear construct such as a *yantra.* Another aid is the labyrinth, effectively drawing the mind to its central source. These techniques may take the mind directly into a trance-like state of great fluidity and receptivity; this is the essence of the center: flowing, non-identified, serene, and blissful.

The basic task of centering is to realize the mind in its natural, "uncreated" state—without form or identification—and actualize it beyond the so-called meditational period.

Before enlightenment,
 chopping wood and carrying water;
After enlightenment,
 chopping wood and carrying water.
Zen proverb

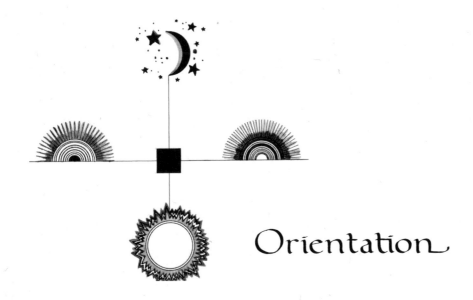

Orientation

Centering naturally creates a coherent and organized field-pattern. The process of creating and realizing this field-pattern is called "orientation." Orientation requires a central position. To witness the rising sun necessitates a point of consciousness which defines itself by the rising sun. From this point the other cardinal points are then defined—East, South, West, and North. This act consecrates. To consecrate is to make sacred, to set apart in the sense of devoting something. The territory of the actual Mandala—whether on the ground, on paper or canvas—is the space on, in and through which the offering and devotion take place. In many of the rituals of the American Indians, the ground on which any conscious act is to occur is consecrated by raising the Sacred Pipe to the six directions (in addition to North, South, East, West, above, and below), and invoking the spirits of these directions:

O our Father, the Sky, hear us and make us strong
O our Mother, the Earth, hear us and give us support
O Spirit of the East, send us your Wisdom
O Spirit of the South, may we tread your Path of Life
O Spirit of the West, may we be always ready for the Long Journey
O Spirit of the North, purify us with your Cleansing Winds.

Orientation may be enacted by dancing as well. In the Tibetan Yoga of Non-Ego, a Dance and Chant of the Five Directions accomplishes the orientation ceremony:

When I beat the drum of Knowledge in the Eastern Continent,
The Heroes and Heroines move around in the Crescent of the Moon;
Their feet flash as they dance upon the prostrate forms of the King Spirits,
Those who symbolize the Demons of Hatred and Wrath.
Let sound the flute of the mirror-like wisdom!

Hum Hum Hum
Phat!

When dancing in the Southern Continent, the Human World,
The Heroes and Heroines move around in the Triangle of Man:
Their feet flash as they dance upon the prostrate head of Pride embodied in
    the Lord of Death.
The Skull-Drums of the Wisdom of Equality,
Let sound with a peculiar sharp tapping sound

Hum Hum Hum
Phat!

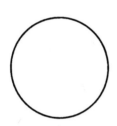

When dancing in the Western Continent, blessed with the Oxen of the Sun,
The Heroes and Heroines move around in the Circle of the Sun
Their feet flash as they dance upon the prostrate head of the Ogress of Lust;
They tinkle the bells of the Discriminating Wisdom in sweet, harmonious tones.

Hum Hum Hum
Phat!

When dancing in the Northern Continent of Unpleasant Sound
The Heroes and Heroines move around in the Square of the Continent of the
    Night;
Their feet flash as they dance upon the prostrate heads of the mischievious
    Sprites of Jealousy;
The Tiara of the All-Fulfilling Wisdom glistens brightly.

Hum Hum Hum
Phat!

When dancing in the Center of the Perfectly Endowed Spot,
The area for the Dance of the Heroes and Heroines is blessed with the influence
    of their Divinity
Their feet flash as they dance upon the prostrate head of the Vampire of
    Ignorance;
The joyous songs of the Wisdom of the Real Essence sounds melodiously.

Hum Hum Hum
Phat!

In this rhythmic ritual the Holy Circle—the Ground of the Mandala—is consecrated. The initiate is at the center and begins to partake of the emanating powers. The Tantric rituals may involve a teacher—*guru.* In the traditions of the American Indians the participants may be a Medicine Man and a patient. The Medicine Man and the *guru* are essentially the same in their roles—their service is to heal and lead to wholeness. And likewise, the initiate and the patient are also one: they are led to a greater integration through a renewed cosmic identification.

The orientation rites emphasize several important factors such as the utilization of the purified body and all its senses. David Villaseñor writes, "The truly successful Medicine Man uses a seemingly hypnotic stimulus consciously directed at the seven major physical glands (or psychic centers) by exciting the activity of the five senses." The Navaho rituals are called "Sings" because of the continual chanting that forms the sound-ground of the ceremony. This is similar to the Tibetan ritual chanting of mantrams, and the use of bells, flutes, and drums. The sense of smell is stimulated by incense, that of taste by the ingesting of certain herbs or teas, and in the American practice, even by the use of hallucinogens such as peyotl. The visual sense is naturally enhanced by the colors and forms that comprise the actual construction of the Mandala as as well as by any prior visualization. The sense of touch and movement is stimulated by dancing, and in some cases, in the Navaho ritual, by the passing of feathers over parts of the patient's body. The outer sensory activation is related to the harmonization of the inner psychic centers or Chakras. The purpose is to bring about a complete psychophysical harmony—a performance of total resonance.

Construction

The actual construction of the Mandala may take different forms—as many forms as there are situations. Certain basic types tend to stand out, and among these we wish to distinguish two fundamental genres: the Mandala as Cosmic Fortress, and the Mandala as the Transmutation of Demonic Forces. The first deals with the projection of the map of the cosmos—a full realization of the entire dynamic cosmogenic processes: the creation of the world systems, ages, seasons, and various cycles of elements and organic hierarchies.

Mandala of Durgatipariśodhana.

In the Beginning there is the End
And this is without Name and Form
From the Formless there comes the Formed
From the Atom of Ether there comes the Atom of Fire
From Fire Air, from Air Water, and from Water
There finally comes the Atom of the Earth
And from the Earth a Crystal, and from this the Mineral Kingdom
And from the Spiralling Dissolution of the Crystal
Comes the Cell, and from the Cell
The Colony, and from the Colony
The Kingdoms of Plants and Animals
And the Kingdom of the Animals is Crowned
By the Kingdom of Man
And Man himself is Crowned with the Tiara
Of Self-Reflective Awareness
By which all these Things may come to be Known
And this Crown, this Tiara of Self-Reflective Awareness
Is itself but the Bottom Rung of the Ladder of Divine Renewal
The Ladder by which the Power of the Eternal
Ascends and meets itself in the Light of the End

In the classical Tibetan Mandala, this cosmogenic process is often conceived of as a palace or fortress of sumptuous appearance and awesome dimensions and levels of defense. Not only is the Mandala literally a cosmic plan, but also a celestial palace. Such Mandalas are the "homes" of the Deity. In the example we have chosen it is the home of *Durgatiparisodhana*—an aspect of *Vairocana*, "The Illuminator." The basic features of this Mandala are: a protective circle comprised of a fire, a *vajra*, and a lotus band; the four portals or gates of the palace; and the inner lotus which is the *bodhi-manda*, the seat of the Deity. On the lotus petals and placed around the inner square are other figures embodying aspects of the Illuminating wisdom. As in Mandalas of this type, the outer protective circle symbolizes "a 'barrier of fire,' which at once prohibits access to the initiate and symbolizes the metaphysical knowledge that 'burns' ignorance."

> *. . . as he approaches its center, the disciple approaches the 'center of the world.' In fact, as soon as he has entered the* mandala, *he is in a sacred space, outside of time; the gods have already 'descended' . . . A series of meditations, for which the disciple has been prepared in advance, help him to find the gods in his own heart. In a vision, he sees them all emerge and spring from his heart; they fill cosmic space, then are reabsorbed in him. In other words, he 'realizes' the eternal process of the periodic creation and destruction of the worlds; and this allows him to enter into the rhythms of the cosmic great time and to understand its emptiness. He shatters the plane of* samsara *and enters a transcendent plane. . ."*

Mircea Eliade

Though much simpler in design, the Navaho sandpainting of the *Four Houses of the Sun*, represents an idea similar to the Tibetan Fortress-type Mandala. (See Plate 7.) The outer circle forms a protective shroud. The opening at the East is watched by the Guardian of the Night, the bat. Within are the four different sun shields, or houses of the sun. Each of these shields has a pair of horns which are of the color traditionally assigned to the station opposite them: the sun shield of the East (Spring) has horns of the color of the West (Autumn); and the North of the South (Summer and Winter, respectively); and vice versa. The interchanged color symbolizes the sense of harmony and cooperation necessary in the functioning of nature as a whole.

Once again the lesson of the opposites: nothing can be defined or exist by itself, but only through its opposite; only when they are mutually supportive can there be a release of creative power between the perpetually generated polar forces. The basic theme of many Mandala rituals is the transformation of destructive energy through harmony of the opposites. In this particular Mandala the transformation is emphasized by the symbol of the eagle feathers tied to the horn tips. These feathers indicate

> ... that in spite of the potentially destructive powers of cyclones, hurricanes, whirlwinds and blizzards (destructive aspects of the four seasons or directions), when men's thoughts are turned to lofty heights, on the wings of prayer, thanking and blessing the infinite power that can display such tremendous energy, with true devotion and sincerety, this power can be re-directed into a positive and creative force.

David Villaseñor

The world views of the Tibetans and the Navahos are highly developed and systematically ordered in comparison with the fragmented world view of the present time. To conceive of the cosmos in the way that they have done presupposes a more integral or holistic disposition than what underlies the modern point of view. For this reason, the second type of Mandala—the Recognition and Transmutation of Demonic Powers—may be a more appropriate initiation or point of departure for the individual in present-day circumstances.

The Mandala of the Transmutation of Demonic Powers requires the painful recognition and acceptance of the existence of negative or demonic forces at work within oneself. Once this difficult task is achieved, what is required is a visualization and projection of these aspects into an ordered whole. The purpose is not to eliminate these forces—that is impossible considering the nature of energy—but as indicated in the Dance of the Five Directions, to recognize and transform them. Ignorance, jealousy, pride, lust, and hatred are the energies to be liberated through transformation. To fully envision the passion or aspect of that which one is most afraid of confronting is the only way to overcoming it. No matter how terrifying or wrathful the projections and visions of our fears may be, they are mind-born products. Fully projected, they no longer cause us fear and terror, but aid us in seeing the nature of reality and guide us in overcoming our own mind-forged manacles.

This type of Mandala is vividly summarized in the Navaho sandpainting of the *Slayer-of-Alien-Gods.* The central figure is the projection of the conqueror of demonic forces who is none other than that itself, consciously transmuted—the *Slayer-of-Alien-Gods.* In the Tibetan tradition he is often *Mahakala,* the Great Black Lord of Transcendent Wisdom, the Devourer of Passions, or the

great figure who surrounds the Wheel of Life—the Devourer of Impermanence. (See plate 9.) The body of the *Slayer-of-Alien-Gods*

> *. . . is covered with armour of flint, lightning and thunder, that he can control and often use with impunity. . . Above his right hand is the symbol of the power to wield the mighty club to produce earthquakes; and in his left hand there are five lightning arrows to perplex the clever minds of men, especially those not having yet gained control of the five senses through prayer and meditation (indicated by five zig-zag lines on his right cheek and on his forehead). The two feathers, one red with black tip, and one white, indicate the ability to use and direct the five senses with the sixth sense of intuition and wisdom, so that this God-like power is never abused, uncontrolled, nor deviated from the Path of Beauty. . . as long as we are children of the earth, it is our sacred duty to refine these five senses with an absolute determination to master them before we become victims of them. . . Spiritually trained Indians and those who learn the secrets of self-mastery move on beyond the five senses into a daily recognition of the eternal and unseen as being as necessary to every human being as daily food.*

David Villaseñor

The Holy Warrior is surrounded by the four eagle figures who aid, protect, and stand on four sections of the Rainbow Guardian, symbol of purity, abundance, and ever-lasting happiness. The eagles, too, are potentially threatening creatures or psychic aspects. Through self-mastery and realization these beings are now consciously employed in the service of the creative forces. The simplicity of the forms and symbols of this sandpainting provide a model or pattern for the integration of the modern individual—that man is a hero and a knower of beauty and strength who can recognize himself as the *Slayer-of-Alien-Gods.*

The *Tibetan Wheel of Life* is another example of the Mandala of the Recognition and Transmutation of Demonic Forces. (See Plate 9.) Originally the *Wheel of Life* was divided into five sections corresponding, in clockwise order from top downward, to the worlds of the gods, beasts, hell, hungry ghosts, and the world of men. Later tradition added a sixth world, that of the Titans, who are in continual strife against the gods. These worlds represent the sum of evolutionary possibilities—none of which is a permanent state.

The center of the *Wheel* depicts a pig, rooster, and serpent, attempting to devour one another. Surrounding these figures is a disc, half white and half black, in which men are represented in various stages of ascending and descending fortune. In the outermost ring are scenes depicting aspects of the twelvefold law of interdependent causation: ignorance, volition, consciousness, mind-body, sense-spheres, contact, feeling, craving, grasping, becoming, birth, old-age-and-death. Embracing the entire wheel is the Devourer of Impermanence—the equivalent of the *Slayer-of-Alien-Gods.* In each of the six realms of beings there is a Buddha figure indicating the possibility for realization or liberation at whatever level or phase of existence.

O Power from where the Sun does come,
Carrying the Spear of All-Embracing Love;
        Heya Hum Hum Hum

O Power Who shines where we always face
Carrying the Spear of Great Compassion;
        Heya Hum Hum Hum

O Power Who rules where the Sun goes down
Carrying the Spear of Great Affection;
        Heya Hum Hum Hum

O Power Who dwells with the Giant of the Night
Carrying the Spear of Great Impartiality;
        Heya Hum Hum Hum

O Power of the Heavens above and the Earth below
O Great Power of the Center Who relates us all
And makes us relatives of all that is
Carrying the Spear of the Illumined Mind

Power of the Perfect Diamond standing on the prostrate heads of the Elements
        of Selfishness
Implanting in their four limbs the transformative Spears,
And in their Hearts the Spear of the Illumined One,
Transfixing them immovably:

Help us to recognize now the Elements of Hatred, Pride, Lust, Jealousy and
        Ignorance that lie within,
Now transferred and transmuted
Into the cardinal points of this Holy Circle
And remain at Peace.

        Heya Hum Hum Hum

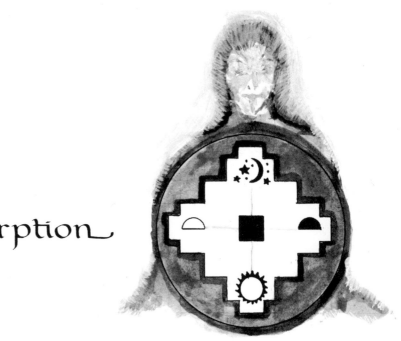

Absorption

Absorption involves intense concentration and meditation upon the completed Mandala so that the contents of the work are transferred to and identified with the mind and body of the beholder. Technically, what occurs is the reabsorption of cosmic forces. In the process of construction these forces were projected out from the chaos of the unconscious; in the process of absorption, the powers are drawn back in again. Prior to the construction there was a relative state of chaos; after the absorption there is a new sense, or state of order. Consciousness has been articulated and expanded. What was relatively unconscious has now been brought to light and raised to a new level, with the consequent increase in light—illumination—for consciousness as a whole.

Often absorption may mean an actual identification of parts or functions of the cosmos with parts or functions of the organism in its cycle of living. Although the center is the unnameable source—neither within nor without—it may be identified with the heart. The solar throne of that center may be the mind, the palaces and pathways leading to that center, the various organs and limbs of the body and its funtions: respiration, circulation, locomotion, and so forth. Directions may denote phases of life or the elemental aspects of the physical organism: blood (water); bones (earth); breath (air); and bodily heat (fire). Whatever way or form the identification takes, it is essential for the beholder/creator to realize that the contents of the Mandala are projections from the various levels of his own conscious life.

In this activity, a fundamental knowledge of certain centers of biopsychic energy or functions is of value. At the simplest level the projections of the Mandala can be related to a head center, heart center, and body center. The actual construction of the Mandala may relate to the individual's mental/intellectual order; the kind and nature of visual projections, their colors and relations to each other may be associated with the individual's emotional center; the over-all pattern may pertain to the body image in general. These ideas are suggested merely to indicate that there must be a total one-to-one coming to terms with the created Mandala.

Since the mental, emotional and bodily activities are in constant interrelation, continually exchanging energies and impinging upon each other, there can be no clear-cut analysis in the process of absorption, but rather an intuitive interfusion of the various parts and functions of both Mandala and organism. The more complete the identification, the more intense and ecstatic is the experience of absorption. To realize the essential unity, the source, the godhead, the fountain of creative energies in and through oneself is the very basis of self-renewal.

Destruction

Following the phase of absorption is destruction, or detachment from the Mandala construction proper. Sandpaintings are very often destroyed at this point. Ceremonies among the Navahos are considered so sacred that outsiders are generally not permitted to attend; and since the sandpainting itself is the ultimate symbol of the sacredness of the particular function, its existence would be profaned if it were not "destroyed" after the ceremony. However, to the Medicine Man or the Yogi, there is no destruction as such. As the body at the time of death is decomposed and returned to a more elemental state—freeing the spirit—so with the sandpainted Mandala which is wiped out and returned to that state whence it came. In one sense, the true spirit has already been released in the process of absorption, and so the essential transformation has occurred in the transfer of the cosmic map to the parts and functions of the body and its cycle of life.

The physical destruction of the Mandala is least significant in the process of following absorption. The chief point to be considered is that of detachment from the created work. Most Mandalas painted on cloth, canvas or paper are not destroyed but hung in a temple, or in some place to create a sacred environment. If the contents of the Mandala have been absorbed, then it is within, and the outer Mandala is only a construct or point of departure.

Detachment is a lesson for the soul not to take pride in the work, nor to view it as another ego-manifestation. The ideal point of view follows from the notion of the openness of all things: there is no actor and no action, though there is acting. The performer is acting only by virtue of his receptivity to the flow of energies coming from the source. The source is not "his" but universal and common to all. Man is a vessel, a mask of the Great Actor, a limb of the Great Dancer. And the work that is performed, though bearing the imprint of the moment as it has passed through the vessel, is but a turn of the Kaleidoscope of Divine Vision.

If the work is not physically destroyed, then its function becomes that of an object of meditation or "remembrance." Its purpose as a daily reminder is to concentrate the mind by recalling for it, its nature, origins, and destiny.

CReintegration

Reintegration is implicit in the very act of projecting and creating the Mandala, but is not insured until detachment has taken place. It is healing or making whole once again through the re-establishment of a direct connection with the Source.

Whatever psychophysical disturbance might have existed prior to the creation of the Mandala has been dissipated and transformed, so that the organism is able to experience itself as a seamless flow of energies. No longer is there a precise division between inner and outer worlds. The very concept of inner and outer is a divisive point of view. Occurrences to the organism, and projections from it are experienced as the beautiful interweavings of a larger whole—an aspect of something yet greater and more mysterious.

What does it mean to be reintegrated, if not to be consciously rewoven into the serpentine path of nature, flowing with and accepting the pattern and course of a greater rhythm than one's reason can measure and protect? To be healthy and to be self-healing, to walk on a Path of Beauty—this is the measure of wholeness.

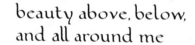

beauty above, below,
and all around me

To be whole is to be willingly and knowingly attuned with the great forces of the universe—to acknowledge, praise, and give thanks to these forces: this is the Path of Beauty. As Villaseñor points out, "The term Beauty Path is a a complete spiritual concept covering the soul experiences and forming a way of life." The rhythm of the Beauty Path is likened to a bird, one of whose wings symbolizes the physical, conscious thinking process; and the other, the spiritual, including the unconscious patterns. The Mandala ritual is a means by which both of these wings may be coordinated and used so that the bird may fly, whole and free.

Actualization

The actual ritual process is only a prelude. Whether destroyed or placed on the wall the Mandala is only a reminder of the on-going mandalic process potential in every living organism, and which relates every creature to the larger web of reality. If the ritual of the Mandala can, in any way, make this truth a living reality within the boundaries of the everyday, then it shall have served its function.

Revealed in the deceptively simple pattern of the spider web is not only the spider's nature, but the eternal web of creation. Man, too, has a web, visible and invisible, which spreads into the recesses of all creation. To articulate and express this web, to let its filaments shine in the morning light of renewed consciousness, to understand the immeasurable and limitless domain which it encompasses, is to pass beyond the restricting border-worlds of birth-and-death. The spider, the butterfly, the flower, and the tree, the snake, the lizard, the squirrel and the bear—these are creatures whose perpetual generation spreads beyond the span of the memory of man. And man remembers not his origins, except through dream and vision, and only then as metaphors spawned from a source beyond reckoning. Unless a man dwells in the conscious precincts of this source, his actions will be like a blind man thrashing in the night, and whether he hits or misses his mark will be a matter of continual debate.

The ritual of the Mandala as devised by the Tantric Yogis of India and Tibet, or the Medicine Men and Shamans of the New World is a means by which men might recover some sense of that life-renewing source. Chaos is, and order is, and both exist simultaneously one within the other. It is only a shift of consciousness that sees in each a reflection of the other. It is this leap —silently and like a prayer—which makes for the vision of wholeness. And it is the vision of wholeness that heals and is self-healing. To live mandalized is to see in chaos the light-shafts of order springing forth from the midnight center, and in every moment and space of time to recognize that it is ourselves we meet mirrored fourfold in the center of every deed.

To actualize the Mandala is to leave the world of fragmentation and alienaation, and pass into another dimension of being, knowing, and doing. All new knowledge comes in the form of an initiation; in restoring to him the means to the source of the vision of the whole, the ritual of the Mandala may give man the knowledge necessary to make the next evolutionary step.

For man must now find in himself the vision to go beyond the world he has created if he is to escape the fate of previously extinct species, and transfigure himself once more into the image of the divine purpose.

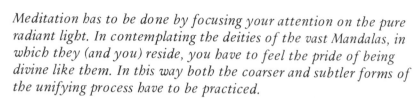

Meditation has to be done by focusing your attention on the pure radiant light. In contemplating the deities of the vast Mandalas, in which they (and you) reside, you have to feel the pride of being divine like them. In this way both the coarser and subtler forms of the unifying process have to be practiced.

Tsong-kha-pa

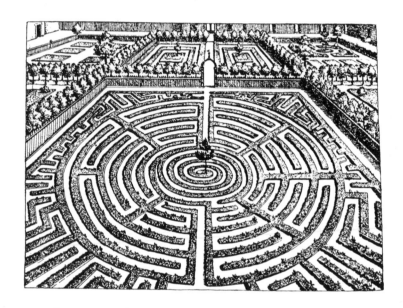

Meditations and Exercises
Cosmic Evocation

Sit in a comfortable position. Close your eyes and slowly take a few deep breaths. Establish your coordinates: in front of you, behind, to the left and right, above and below. Try to feel them within a radius of four feet from your your body. Experience, if you can, the points on your body with which these coordinates touch, and in your body where they all meet. Relate these co-ordinates to the cardinal directions.

Then, in your mind's eye, visualize a circle. It may be open or full. Hold this image steadily in your mind's eye. If extraneous thoughts occur, you may ask: "To whom are these thoughts occurring?" And if the answer is "To me,"

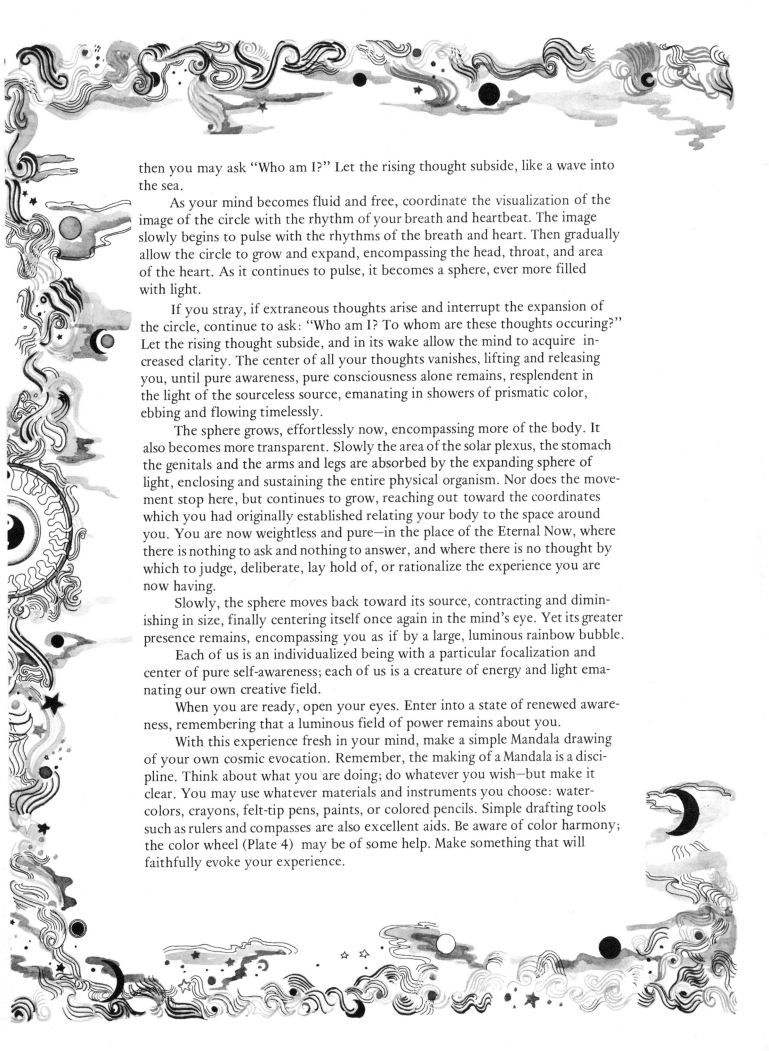

then you may ask "Who am I?" Let the rising thought subside, like a wave into the sea.

As your mind becomes fluid and free, coordinate the visualization of the image of the circle with the rhythm of your breath and heartbeat. The image slowly begins to pulse with the rhythms of the breath and heart. Then gradually allow the circle to grow and expand, encompassing the head, throat, and area of the heart. As it continues to pulse, it becomes a sphere, ever more filled with light.

If you stray, if extraneous thoughts arise and interrupt the expansion of the circle, continue to ask: "Who am I? To whom are these thoughts occuring?" Let the rising thought subside, and in its wake allow the mind to acquire increased clarity. The center of all your thoughts vanishes, lifting and releasing you, until pure awareness, pure consciousness alone remains, resplendent in the light of the sourceless source, emanating in showers of prismatic color, ebbing and flowing timelessly.

The sphere grows, effortlessly now, encompassing more of the body. It also becomes more transparent. Slowly the area of the solar plexus, the stomach the genitals and the arms and legs are absorbed by the expanding sphere of light, enclosing and sustaining the entire physical organism. Nor does the movement stop here, but continues to grow, reaching out toward the coordinates which you had originally established relating your body to the space around you. You are now weightless and pure—in the place of the Eternal Now, where there is nothing to ask and nothing to answer, and where there is no thought by which to judge, deliberate, lay hold of, or rationalize the experience you are now having.

Slowly, the sphere moves back toward its source, contracting and diminishing in size, finally centering itself once again in the mind's eye. Yet its greater presence remains, encompassing you as if by a large, luminous rainbow bubble.

Each of us is an individualized being with a particular focalization and center of pure self-awareness; each of us is a creature of energy and light emanating our own creative field.

When you are ready, open your eyes. Enter into a state of renewed awareness, remembering that a luminous field of power remains about you.

With this experience fresh in your mind, make a simple Mandala drawing of your own cosmic evocation. Remember, the making of a Mandala is a discipline. Think about what you are doing; do whatever you wish—but make it clear. You may use whatever materials and instruments you choose: watercolors, crayons, felt-tip pens, paints, or colored pencils. Simple drafting tools such as rulers and compasses are also excellent aids. Be aware of color harmony; the color wheel (Plate 4) may be of some help. Make something that will faithfully evoke your experience.

Simple Yantra

For the following exercise, limit yourself to three forms—the circle, square, and and equilateral triangle—in whatever numbers, sizes and sets of relationships.

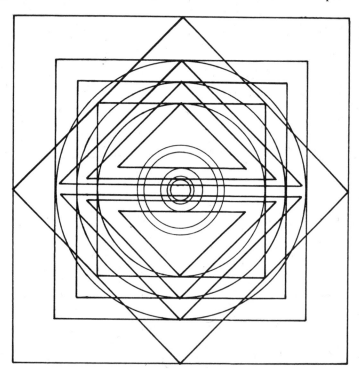

The *yantra* is a vehicle for concentrating the mind; it is literally a practical meditation. Meditate briefly on each of the forms prior to doing the exercise. In other words, first meditate on the circle; be aware of your associations, and whatever colors may appear. Do the same with the triangle and the square. The basic idea behind the *yantra* is the disciplining of the mind, and the creation of a fundamental map of harmony. Limit yourself to what seems necessary in accordance with your sets of associations with the forms. If you use colors, be aware of color harmony and contrast.

Cycle-of-Life Mandala

This is a much more intricate and introspectively demanding kind of exercise. It can be worked out on a number of different levels of personal development, covering various periods of time simultaneously. At the simplest level, consider the passage of a day divided into two parts, from sunrise to sunset and sunset to sunrise. Within this bipolar arrangement you may consider the nature of your activity—psychic and actual—within each of the two spheres. Project these fields of activity in terms of simple symbols and/or colors. Introspect and see if there is a particular rhythmic quality to each of the two spheres. The important point is to simplify and project the most basic qualities in order to develop a symbolic awareness. Although you might have begun with a consideration of the bipolar rhythm of a day in your life, that rhythm, when symbolically perceived and appreciated, may be seen to extend to a basic statement about life-and-death itself.

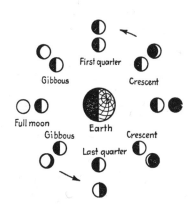

Or, you may be led from a simple division to a triple or quartenary division of the day. If a fourfold division of your day seems the most natural approach, extend that division to the seasons of the year, or to the organic phases of the life cycle itself. The Mandala of the fourfold division of the daily cycle naturally emphasizes the square and all its ramifications and associations. Once again, the significant function of these meditation practices is the development of symbolic awareness—the more correspondences between the rhythms of the daily cycle of your life and the various larger cycles, the greater is your attunement to a larger harmony.

What appear to be personal problems and vexations may be seen as functions of a natural rhythm—there is always a great relief and sense of liberation in realizing that we are a part of a natural flow and that we partake without effort of the perturbations and ecstasies of that flow. Keep a meditational journal of Mandalas and related observations. The record of Mandalas that you establish may also become a reminder of the purpose and way of natural harmony.

Although we have suggested double and fourfold daily Mandalas, you should not feel limited or restricted to these: six-, eight-, nine-, twelve-, and twenty-fourfold Mandalas are equally suggestive for a beginning—the Mandala is infinite, as are the capacities of the individual.

Group Mandalas

The purpose of individual Mandalas is to establish a sense of harmony within, so that the individual may turn himself outward with greater selflessness, clarity, compassion and joy, knowing through his work that he is but a part of the larger stream. The purpose of the group Mandala is to achieve this through a network of individuals functioning as an organic whole.

Two or more people may work on a given project; they may achieve their ends in two different ways: by working parallel with little interaction, achieving piecemeal what must be done; or, through an interactive network of activities in which there is a continual conscious process of sharing, giving and taking. The latter method is the way of the group Mandala.

The Mandala of two offers unique possibilities, particularly for couples. The male/female relationship is prone to the pitfalls of polarization, and today presents a microcosm of the confusion regarding the nature of sex and being human. If there is something of a war of the sexes, it can only mean that a basic understanding concerning the essential unity of things has disintegrated, and that an extreme state of polarization is upon us.

A simple Mandala involving two people of opposite sex may be most fruitful in exploring this whole question—to see if two creatures can breathe a unified vision. Special attention should be paid to matters of procedure—who initiates, who does what and in what manner or way; does one person do all the planning and the other all the "filling in?" What kinds of colors and forms do each use, and do they try to harmonize these forms and colors? Harmonization does not mean the loss of individual uniqueness—women are women and men are men, I am I and you are you. Rather, the process of harmonization brings together self-rooted individuals, independently working together to create a new, organic whole.

Through such an exercise the couple may come to appreciate and better understand the deeper significance of the *Yab-Yum* images which figure so prominently in Tantric Mandalas and devotional works. The *Yab-Yum*—which literally means "father-mother"—represents the act of sexual union as the symbol *par excellence* of unity, or more specifically, of divine reunion. It is a union of wisdom and skillful means—the coming together of the heart and the mind.

This Mandala exercise can be just as meaningful for a single person of either sex, since no one is entirely male or female, but a blend of both.

> *The human person . . . is a coexistence of two opposing tendencies, the one centrifugal and the other centripetal, thus as the one tendency leads us out of ourselves, the other guides us towards the return, towards the central point, the undecaying condition. . .*
> Tucci

The Divine Androgyne is that creature who has been able to realize both of the sexes within himself. It may also be thought of as the symbolic image of the union of male and female elements by a couple.

The union of the sexes—the ultimate aspects of the opposites as they manifest in the human world—is a major point of departure for all group Mandalas. Because of the critical situation today regarding the sexes and polarization in general, we may only caution that if group Mandalas are done with more than two people, that it involve an already existing group. A Mandala by itself cannot create an integrally related couple, family or group; it can, however, serve to explore, strengthen, and intensify what already exists.

Notes

In addition to the previously mentioned works of Tucci, *Theory and Practice of the Mandala;* Eliade, *Yoga: Immortality and Freedom;* Villasenor, *Tapestries in Sand;* and Brown, *The Sacred Pipe;* ideas and descriptions of the nature of ritual and the ritual practices involving the Mandala are found in: Mai-Mai Sze, *The Way of Chinese Painting* (New York: Vintage Books, 1959); W.Y. Evans-Wentz, *The Tibetan Book of the Great Liberation* (New York: Oxford University Press, 1968), particularly Book II, "The Yoga of Knowing the Mind," pp. 195-240; and by the same author, *Tibetan Yoga and Secret Doctrines* (New York: Oxford University Press, 1958), Book V, "The Path of the Mystic Sacrifice," pp. 279-334; Jean Eracle, *L'art des thanka et le buddhisme tantrique* (Geneva: Musee d'ethnographie, 1970); Herbert V. Guenther, *Treasures on the Tibetan Middle Way* (Berkeley: Shambala Publications, 1969); and C.A. Muses, *Esoteric Teachings of the Tibetan Tantra* (Indian Hills, Colorado: Falcon's Wing Press, 1961).

The Monster Mask (page 83) is reprinted from the *Catalogue of the Tibetan Collection,* Volumes I & II (Newark Museum, 1971). "Mandala of Durgatiparisodhana" is from *A New Tibeto-Mongol Pantheon,* Part 12, by Professors Raghu Vira and Lokesh Chandra (International Academy of Indian Culture, New Delhi, 1967). Chant of the Five Directions is adapted from *Tibetan Yoga and Secret Doctrines: Seven Books of Wisdom of the Great Path,* arranged and edited by W. Y. Evans-Wentz. © W.Y. Evans-Wentz, 1958. Reprinted by permission of Oxford University Press, Inc.

And Through the Sun Beyond

What Even Man Or
Flower Knows

VI
The Mandala as Point of Departure

It is only under ideal conditions, when life is still simple and unconscious enough to follow the serpentine path of instinct without hesitation or misgiving, that the compensating function of the unconscious works with entire success. The more civilized ...and complicated a man is, the less he is able to follow his instincts. His complicated living conditions and the influence of his environment are so strong that they drown the quiet voice of nature. Opinions, beliefs, theories, and collective tendencies appear in its stead and back up all the aberrations of the conscious mind...   Carl G. Jung

A tremendous gulf exists between the ritual of the Mandala and the actualities of present-day living. If it is a person's avowed task to transit from a state of profane to one of sacred living, there could scarcely be a more difficult endeavor. Profane living is at the expense of the whole, fragmented and alienated. Sacred living is not simply a return to the "serpentine path of instinct," but is rooted in the source of wholeness and spreads outward as the flower from the stem.

The mandalization of man is a process by which the polarities of individualism and collectivism are united, creating a distinct synthesis. As a single person begins to see, realize and understand himself as a unique reflection and repository of the forces and energies of the whole of nature—man the conscious microcosm—so he then begins to act as an agent releasing radiant energies and attracting other beings and energies toward him. He becomes a conscious center. The attraction he exerts is not to create a system of satellites about him, but to instill this realization in others, so that all may hold together as conscious centers, each with a unique function and universal awareness and capacity for further transformation. The collective strength of the Mandala is made possible by the self-defined and mutually self-accepted differentiation of the indviduals which comprise it.

The individualism which has flourished in recent centuries is a preparation. It can be likened to new shoots springing forth out of the earth. Having burst out of the germinating darkness for the first time, there is a feeling—illusory as it may be—of aggressive strength and pride—a domineering attitude that has

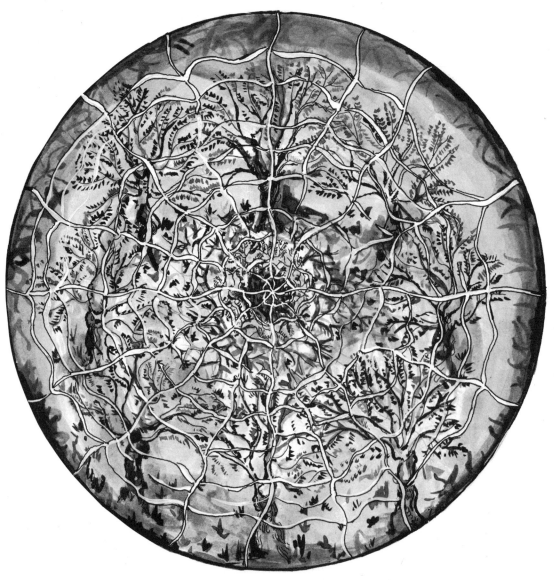

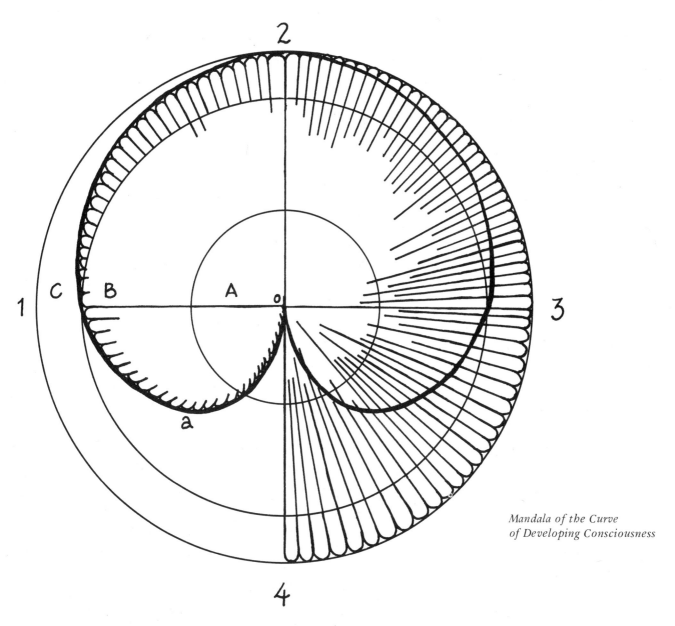

Mandala of the Curve
of Developing Consciousness

meaning only in relation to the preceding state. As with all living organisms, so with the new shoots that are one day to comprise the intricate web of the living forest. The hard energy of the arousing strength necessary to push through the earth in time becomes yielding and resilient. So it is in the present stage of humanity. The individualism fostered by recent human development has reached ever outward, internalizing sense and feeling behind the cloak of reason. It has stretched to the very limits of human endurance, all too often at the expense of that knowledge and experience of the source by which the exertion of such energy is possible in the first place.

The *Mandala of the Curve of Developing Consciousness* sets forth the nature of the present situation within a larger context. Our main concern is to indicate how this curve operates at the individual as well as the larger global level. There are always exceptions, and our description is to be understood in the most general terms.

The overall form consists of three circles concentrically arranged. The innermost circle—A—is the domain of core consciousness, the most basic and vital area in which the primordial evolutionary impulses are contained. It is the least accessible to voluntary control and corresponds to the deepest cortical portions of the brain, including the medulla oblongata, the vital center for breathing, circulation, and autonomous nervous functions. The core zone recapitulates the earliest evolutionary phases of life—from this level emanate the most fundamental animistic visions and hallucinations.

The second circle—B—represents the intermediate or collective level of consciousness—what Jung would call the collective unconscious. This zone is the repository of all the ideas, dreams, myths, symbols, and archetypes immediately accessible for human implementation. It also represents a developmental accretion of collective experiences—though possibly all of the experiences of the human species do not really add to this realm, but rather are manifestations of impulses which originate here. Through an effort of will the contents of this zone may reveal themselves.

The third and outermost circle—C—is the zone of surface consciousness. This is the level of maximum differentiation of phenomena, the realm of 'everyday' or what is usually called 'waking' consciousness. It is the level at which volitional actions are most common, and in which the ego has most 'control.'

These three circles may be considered as a single unit, the ideal being an operating integration of the three levels or zones of consciousness. The actual development of consciousness is represented by a line—a—curving outward from the center. This center is represented by o, and indicates the first manifestations of consciousness—that core of life shared in common by plants, animals, and man. The force plunging through the center of the Mandala originates beyond, in another dimension.

The curve between o and 1 represents the development of consciousness through the earliest phases of life, and most specifically through the tribal/collective stages of the human community—what many myths and histories refer to as the Golden Age. Point 1 indicates the place at which the curve breaks through from the collective levels of tribal consciousness to the beginning of individual self-awareness. From 1 to 2 the curve charts the development of consciousness through the individualist stages of culture to a point of maximum individualism. In contrast to the earlier phase, the activity of consciousness now tends to concentrate more in the surface zone of greater differentiation, and less in the zone of collective consciousness.

In the collective/tribal stage all acts are related to a particular cosmic order; in the individualizing phase the basic frame of reference is an historical development which culminates in the extension of consciousness to an awareness of the globe as a whole. This period includes the great migrations, the rise of the world religions, the great revolutions, and world wars, which are the distinguishing features of the outward push of consciousness. Historically the beginning of this development at point 1 may correspond to the time around 600 B.C. with the appearance of Gautama Buddha, Pythagoras, and Lao Tzu, the first of the great spiritual teachers whose traditions extend through Christ, Muhammed and Baha 'ullah. The conclusion of this phase may already have occurred by the nineteenth century, which saw the rise and extension of individualism and materialism on a world-wide scale.

Point 2 on our chart indicates the limit of individual self-awareness, and the beginning of the path of integration. This marks a fundamental reorienta-

tion and inward turn of the curve of developing consciousness. The curve between points 2 and 3 represents the development through the individuating and unitive phases of human culture. Individualism as such is de-emphasized, becoming subordinated to the effort of achieving integrated beings capable of effecting a global unification. Conscious activity turns once more to the collective level. This return does not need to be understood as a loss of differentiation, but may be compared to the plant: in order to push upward to the light, its roots must sink deep into the earth.

The beginning of collective individuation occurs at point 3. The curve of consciousness returns to the intermediate zone, and the individual is firmly based once again in the deeper levels of consciousness. He is no longer uprooted as he was through the phase of developing individualism, but is now a mature organism capable of utilizing all of his potential. At this point, such individuated beings are not the exception, as they have been for the last twenty-five hundred years, but the rule. Without a doubt, this development is still some distance in the future. The collective appearance of a race of individuated human beings will inaugurate the development of integrative culture—represented by the curve between points 3 and 4. Once again there will be a Golden Age, one which integrates the activities of the planet on a global scale.

The re-establishment of harmony, a state of union/liberation—will mean an entry into a new dimension, for which a Mandala such as this will no longer suffice. As is true of all mandalic processes, the end is both a return to the center—or beginning point—and a simultaneous expansion beyond the periphery of what can now be defined or conceived. The actual process of the developing of consciousness is both an exploration and definition of the intermediate and peripheral zones so that a return may be embarked upon.

In our Mandala the activity of consciousness is represented by a series of looped lines running perpendicular to the curve of consciousness. From point o to the zenith, point 2, the processes of consciousness remain within the curve. As this activity moves farther away from the core, especially through the individualizing phases, there is a growing sense of cultural uprootedness—a common feature of technological societies. From this follows the paradox of individualism: a sense of self-awareness accompanied by an increasing feeling of alienation.

Only when self-awareness reaches its limit, does a process of individuation become consciously manifest. At the beginning point of individuation, 2, the activity of consciousness extends above as well as below the curve. Individuation is the process of a greater integration of self-awareness with the deeper levels of consciousness. Though the individuated person is aware of his uniqueness, it is no longer a cause of anguish and alienation. Equally aware of his oneness with all beings, and having re-established his roots in the depths of consciousness, he is able to provide himself a base from which to explore and expand with greater equilibrium. His acts become invested with meaning, and his courage and confidence as an individual entity become all-embracing. This is the birth of the Whole Man.

If the developmental process is an inexorable part of a larger organic whole, then we must seek the seeds of change within the silent mutations of individuals slowly being transformed into individuated beings. We have spoken of this process as "mandalization"—the sinking of the reflective roots of the mind into the core of being, bringing forth a renewed vision of man's place and the nature of creative living within the order of the universe as a whole. For this to happen there must first be an awareness of the present situation in its totality. It may come in a dream or a vision, or only as a slow dawning. However it happens it will be understood and felt as an inner impulse, a voice from within suggesting some other way—perhaps altogether different from what is now conceivable.

The Four Armed Sun-God, painted by a patient under Jungian analysis.

The unconscious coming into being of the Mandala is a symbol of health and wholeness. This process, as we have indicated, has been most fully documented by Carl G. Jung, who has written of and reproduced Mandalas created by his patients. Many of these Mandalas, so simple and striking, bear an irrefutable resemblance to archetypal images from earlier religious and symbolic systems, testifying to the creative reality of the collective unconscious and the potentially unified mind of man.

Mandalas made during the quest for self-healing may be seen as the first impulses of a larger, collective will to wholeness, slowly and sporadically manifesting throughout the rational jungle of twentieth century life. They are random borings into the long-neglected depths of the "irrational." In the last decade, especially since the fall of Tibet in 1959, the reappearance of the Mandala has begun to take on a more conscious character. Recent interest in meditation, yoga, and altered states of consciousness in general, have brought the Mandala to a renewed cultural prominence.

As the vision quest of individuals expanding their awareness deepens, Mandalas reflecting a new spiritual growth are evoked and produced. They are painted markers opening doors to new journeys and possibilities for being. In some cases the creation of and meditation upon the perfection of the Mandala has led to a search for new structures for living. To express the transcendent intuition, some have explored new techniques of light for the creation of that greater depth revealing the interplay of images which often lead to and are called forth by spiritual awakening. For others, the painting of Mandalas has become a pilgrimage through the archetypes and structures of consciousness There are those who have even found that "painted cakes do not satisfy hunger," and have entered more intensely into the arduous mission of transmitting what cannot be expressed in words—or images. The visions we reproduce testify to the reopening of spiritual gates within walls of steel, concrete, and glass.

Awake, awake, O sleeper of the land of shadows,

wake !

Expand !   William Blake

In the present struggle of the planet the mandala presents itself as the seed-symbol of a more harmonized world-order. At the nadir of the cycle of the the involution of the spirit, the source-root has been sparked again. The vision of renewed wholeness and brotherhood slowly spreads and filters through the consciousness of the race. Though only a seed at the moment, it is the seed of the inevitable, and though invisible to our eyes, this seed is already the center of a Mandala as promising of unity and spiritual exaltation as any vision from man's remotest past.

Einstein, prophet of the redemption of matter, declared: "There is no logical way to the discovery of these elementary laws. There is only the way of intuition." As we have extended our vision outward to the stars, so it is now expanding inward encompassing the matrices of intuition. What lies before us is as difficult to conceive from a rationalistic point of view as the scientific era might have been to our ancestors in the cloistered abbeys of the medieval period. But with the expanded eye and senses of intuition the awakened traveller may have little difficulty perceiving in the precincts of tomorrow the fourfold palace of human wisdom built on the Mandala of human brotherhood.

Ａnd every part of the city is fourfold, and every inhabitant fourfold.
Ａnd every pot and vessel and garment and utensil of the houses,
Ａnd every house, fourfold.

William Blake

As a prophet in the midst of the "Mills of Satan," William Blake foresaw—and remembered the Mandala of the fourfold vision of Jerusalem. This is the city of the future which is the eternal city of vision.

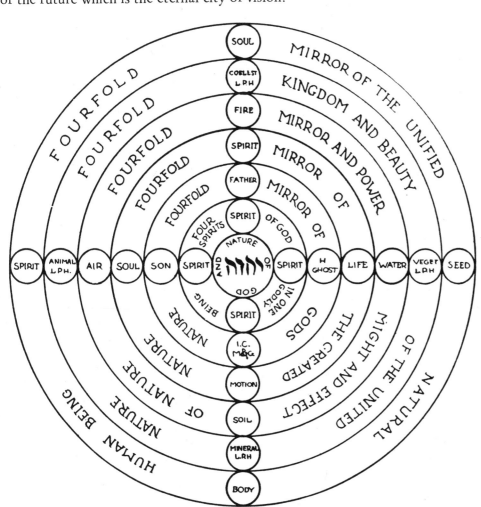

Another modern prophet, the great Sioux seer, Black Elk, also foresaw the fourfold Mandala of human brotherhood:

Then I was standing on the highest mountain of all, and round about beneath me was the whole hoop of the world. And while I stood there I saw more than I can tell and I understood more than I saw; for I was seeing in a sacred manner the shapes of all things in the Spirit, and the shape of all shapes as they must live together like one being. And I saw that the sacred hoop of my people was one of many hoops that made one circle, wide as daylight and as starlight, and in the center grew one mighty flowering tree to shelter all the children of one mother and one father. And I saw that it was holy.

Then as I stood there, two men were coming from the east, head first like arrows flying, and between them rose the day-break star. They came and gave a herb to me and said: 'With this on earth you shall undertake anything and do it.' It was the day-break-star herb, the herb of understanding, and they told me to drop it on the earth. I saw it falling far and when it struck the earth it rooted and grew and flowered, four blossoms on one stem, a blue, a white, a scarlet, and a yellow; and the rays from these streamed upward to the the heavens so that all creatures saw it and in no place was there darkness.

But the path to this vision is painful and full of tragedy. Following the massacre at Wounded Knee, which marked the end, for all practical purposes, of the Indian nations in America, Black Elk spoke for the human race: "There is no center any longer, and the sacred tree is dead." Within ourselves we slowly make the return. Each man who lives must go to the dark center and be reborn. We are the darkened dream of beyond; we are the shadow of the dream that falls across the earth.

Though the Mandala is a universal constant, it is also an act of faith, and an integral part of a personal vision quest. The authors have pursued the way of the Mandala for scarcely more than five years. In these years the vision has taken root and expanded beyond our original thoughts and motivations. As students of history and culture, we had been familiar with the Mandala as an art form of the Orient. But it was only after working through some of the outer coatings of culture and personality, that the creative strength of the center was suddenly manifest to us. Spinning out from the stream-of-consciousness among swirls and eddies of strange and animated figures, symbols, and half-remembered signs, the diamond center of the Mandala slowly took over our drawings and paintings. Following the rhythm of the "serpentine path," we discovered a greater ordering principle—more deeply rooted than any memory. Having evoked from our own need the unifying vision of the Mandala, we began to experience a restored equilibrium. With this came faith that in man and through man himself is the way of transformation.

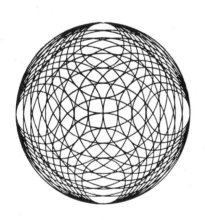

We learned to work together, sharing our insights and discoveries. We experimented merging our energies into one consciousness by painting simultaneously on the same work, often trading positions and paintbrushes. Our experience was that group consciousness is only as strong as the degree of individuation achieved by its members. The way beyond the present impasse of consciousness is only through the individual.

The individual is a path.

Man only matters who takes the path. Saint-Exupery

Rooted in a sense of individual unity within ourselves, we were slowly becoming an organism with two unique centers nourished by one source. A Mandala greater than anything we could express in paint had begun to evolve.

115

Two paintings expressing discoveries in our initial exploration of the **Mandala** are *Mandala of the Octave* (see Plate 11) and *Circulation of the Light* (see **Plate** 12). One is distinctly male, the other female, though neither is completely both. They were worked on simultaneously over a period of about three months. From here the Mandala was to lead to other paths and systems, and at no time since have we worked so exclusively in such precisely formal Mandalas of this scale.

Mandala of the Octave

The original inspiration of the *Octave* was an intuition that I felt keenly to my innermost being, to the point of ecstatic rapture. If all is energy, and the basic quality of energy is a radiant joy, then the universe itself is fundamentally a joyous song, full and incandescent, filling every last atom with the reverberations of a tremendous, creative surge. As I worked and moved with this idea, my faith grew firm, and a conviction of that light which permeates all things gave me a self-renewing strength. Even if the world were lost in the tides of affliction, I knew at the very core that sorrow is only a transition between ignorance and illumination. Underlying even the basest acts and forms is the redeeming flow of an eternally self-transformative energy.

This intuition of the sourceless energy flow was complemented by a deep, underlying sense of structure. Though boundless, energy maintains itself by continual reformulation. Its structure is not necessarily fixed or permanent, though it may have universal aspects and correspondences. During this time study of the *I Ching* provided a corresponding vision of the laws and ways by which the fundamental energy structures itself. Out of the arrangements of the the *pa kua*, I perceived the central form of the octave: the octagon, which is echoed in the painting from the center outward through a dense profusion of energy fields. The form of the octagon is not absolute, but a metaphor for the primordial structuring tendency.

In its intricate abundance of color and form, the Mandala is predominantly *yang*—the only negative space being provided by the octave mirror. The painting marks the end of a period of exploration and fulfillment of my maleness—

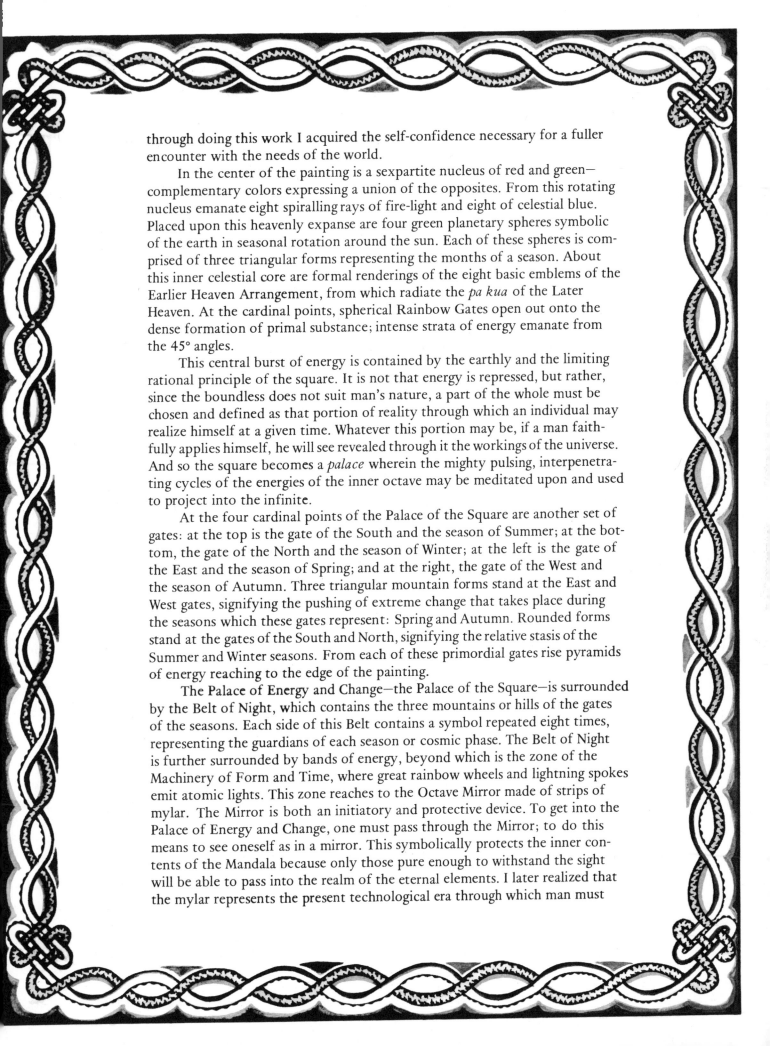

through doing this work I acquired the self-confidence necessary for a fuller encounter with the needs of the world.

In the center of the painting is a sexpartite nucleus of red and green—complementary colors expressing a union of the opposites. From this rotating nucleus emanate eight spiralling rays of fire-light and eight of celestial blue. Placed upon this heavenly expanse are four green planetary spheres symbolic of the earth in seasonal rotation around the sun. Each of these spheres is comprised of three triangular forms representing the months of a season. About this inner celestial core are formal renderings of the eight basic emblems of the Earlier Heaven Arrangement, from which radiate the *pa kua* of the Later Heaven. At the cardinal points, spherical Rainbow Gates open out onto the dense formation of primal substance; intense strata of energy emanate from the 45° angles.

This central burst of energy is contained by the earthly and the limiting rational principle of the square. It is not that energy is repressed, but rather, since the boundless does not suit man's nature, a part of the whole must be chosen and defined as that portion of reality through which an individual may realize himself at a given time. Whatever this portion may be, if a man faithfully applies himself, he will see revealed through it the workings of the universe. And so the square becomes a *palace* wherein the mighty pulsing, interpenetrating cycles of the energies of the inner octave may be meditated upon and used to project into the infinite.

At the four cardinal points of the Palace of the Square are another set of gates: at the top is the gate of the South and the season of Summer; at the bottom, the gate of the North and the season of Winter; at the left is the gate of the East and the season of Spring; and at the right, the gate of the West and the season of Autumn. Three triangular mountain forms stand at the East and West gates, signifying the pushing of extreme change that takes place during the seasons which these gates represent: Spring and Autumn. Rounded forms stand at the gates of the South and North, signifying the relative stasis of the Summer and Winter seasons. From each of these primordial gates rise pyramids of energy reaching to the edge of the painting.

The Palace of Energy and Change—the Palace of the Square—is surrounded by the Belt of Night, which contains the three mountains or hills of the gates of the seasons. Each side of this Belt contains a symbol repeated eight times, representing the guardians of each season or cosmic phase. The Belt of Night is further surrounded by bands of energy, beyond which is the zone of the Machinery of Form and Time, where great rainbow wheels and lightning spokes emit atomic lights. This zone reaches to the Octave Mirror made of strips of mylar. The Mirror is both an initiatory and protective device. To get into the Palace of Energy and Change, one must pass through the Mirror; to do this means to see oneself as in a mirror. This symbolically protects the inner contents of the Mandala because only those pure enough to withstand the sight will be able to pass into the realm of the eternal elements. I later realized that the mylar represents the present technological era through which man must pass and face himself as he actually is, if he wishes to re-establish communion with the core of energy which lies within.

Surrounding the Octave Mirror is a large, all-encompassing Rainbow Circle —the celestial kaleidoscope of decomposed white light, symbolic of the essence. At the four corners of the painting proper, are four energy semi-circles opening onto other universes, radiant and beyond expression. The entire *Mandala of the Octave* is essentially an infinitely repeatable module, just as the octave in music. Though I speak of it as infinitely repeatable, its contents are infinitely changeable.

A physicist once remarked that this Mandala reminded him of a basic form in quantum mechanics. Whether it is an allusion to modern physics, to music, to the eight symbols of Change, or to the Eightfold Wheel of the Law— the Wheel of the Dharma—it makes little difference. If, from the point of view of modern physics, the universe is not necessarily matter, but music, then the dream of the poet is as valid as the roar of the locomotive, and the Wheel of the Law turned by the Buddha still resonates amidst the hum and clackety-whirr of mechanized gears. What changes and what remains the same?

When you fix your heart on one point,
then nothing is impossible for you.
Buddha

Circulation of the Light

Circulation of the Light is a manifestation of an energy complementary to that described above by José This is not to place a template of duality upon our works. Every opposition becomes a part of a larger, complementary process, once the life pattern of birth-and-death is recognized.

Through such reflections I slowly experienced the ways in which my own being resonated with the Mandala and its principles of organicity and wholeness. This was and is not an easy task. The process of mandalizing occurs not only at moments of meditation, but is woven into the very fabric of the daily rhythm—waking, sleeping, breathing, loving, painting, speaking, washing dishes. . .

During these explorations of the Mandala, I read *Secret of the Golden Flower,* and became absorbed in the sections dealing with "the circulation of the light." I felt a deep kinship with what I read—its source and mine seemed to be one. I was going through a rite of passage—the initiation into the Mandala. Though far from any traditional Mandala ritual, the rite was born out of neces-sity, and was absolutely appropriate for my situation.

I visualized the mutual dependence of heart and breath and realized that the circulation of the light must become united with the pattern of breathing.

*The light is not in the body alone, nor is it only outside the body.
Mountains and rivers and the great earth are lit by the sun and moon,
and all that is this light. Therefore it is not only within the body.
Understanding and clarity, perception and enlightenment, and all
movements (of the spirit) are likewise this light. . .*

*The lightflower of heaven and earth fills all the thousand spaces.
But also the lightflower of the individual body passes through heaven
and covers the earth. Therefore, as soon as the light is circulating,
heaven and earth, mountains and rivers, all are circulating at the same
time.*

Secret of the Golden Flower

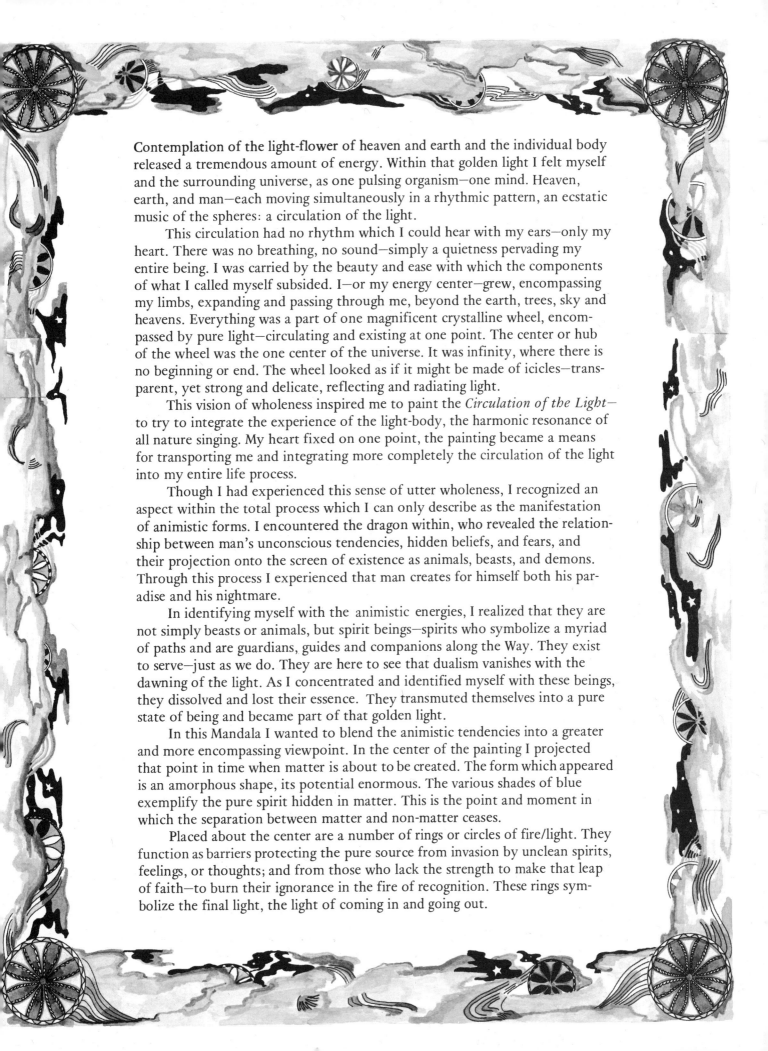

Contemplation of the light-flower of heaven and earth and the individual body released a tremendous amount of energy. Within that golden light I felt myself and the surrounding universe, as one pulsing organism—one mind. Heaven, earth, and man—each moving simultaneously in a rhythmic pattern, an ecstatic music of the spheres: a circulation of the light.

This circulation had no rhythm which I could hear with my ears—only my heart. There was no breathing, no sound—simply a quietness pervading my entire being. I was carried by the beauty and ease with which the components of what I called myself subsided. I—or my energy center—grew, encompassing my limbs, expanding and passing through me, beyond the earth, trees, sky and heavens. Everything was a part of one magnificent crystalline wheel, encompassed by pure light—circulating and existing at one point. The center or hub of the wheel was the one center of the universe. It was infinity, where there is no beginning or end. The wheel looked as if it might be made of icicles—transparent, yet strong and delicate, reflecting and radiating light.

This vision of wholeness inspired me to paint the *Circulation of the Light*—to try to integrate the experience of the light-body, the harmonic resonance of all nature singing. My heart fixed on one point, the painting became a means for transporting me and integrating more completely the circulation of the light into my entire life process.

Though I had experienced this sense of utter wholeness, I recognized an aspect within the total process which I can only describe as the manifestation of animistic forms. I encountered the dragon within, who revealed the relationship between man's unconscious tendencies, hidden beliefs, and fears, and their projection onto the screen of existence as animals, beasts, and demons. Through this process I experienced that man creates for himself both his paradise and his nightmare.

In identifying myself with the animistic energies, I realized that they are not simply beasts or animals, but spirit beings—spirits who symbolize a myriad of paths and are guardians, guides and companions along the Way. They exist to serve—just as we do. They are here to see that dualism vanishes with the dawning of the light. As I concentrated and identified myself with these beings, they dissolved and lost their essence. They transmuted themselves into a pure state of being and became part of that golden light.

In this Mandala I wanted to blend the animistic tendencies into a greater and more encompassing viewpoint. In the center of the painting I projected that point in time when matter is about to be created. The form which appeared is an amorphous shape, its potential enormous. The various shades of blue exemplify the pure spirit hidden in matter. This is the point and moment in which the separation between matter and non-matter ceases.

Placed about the center are a number of rings or circles of fire/light. They function as barriers protecting the pure source from invasion by unclean spirits, feelings, or thoughts; and from those who lack the strength to make that leap of faith—to burn their ignorance in the fire of recognition. These rings symbolize the final light, the light of coming in and going out.

Plate 11: *Mandala of the Octave.* José Argüelles.

Plate 12: *Circulation of the Light*. Miriam Argüelles.

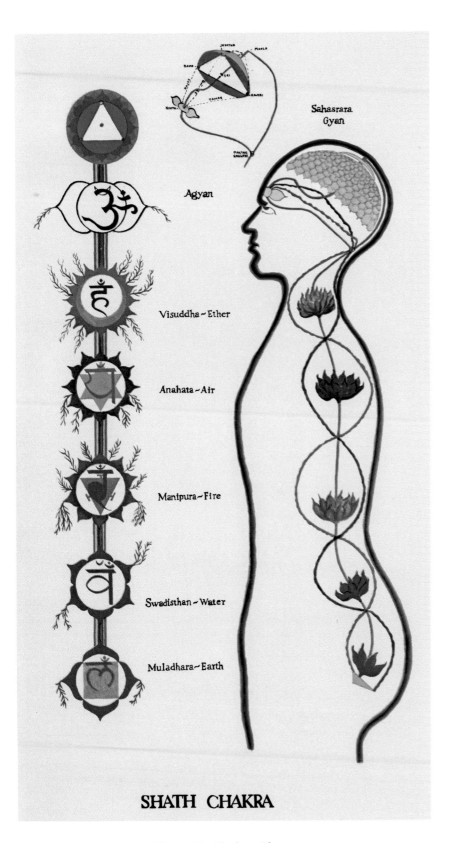

Sahasrara
Gyan

Agyan

Visuddha ~ Ether

Anahata ~ Air

Manipura ~ Fire

Swadisthan ~ Water

Muladhara ~ Earth

SHATH CHAKRA

Plate 13. *Chakra Chart.*
Plate 14: *In order for there to be new birth, the Mage must move across the earth.* José and Miriam Argüelles.

Plate 15:
Radiant Woman.
José Argüelles.

Plate 16:
Radiant Man.
Miriam Argüelles

The colorful fire rings form the outer core of the center of the eight pointed star. Placed at the cardinal points of the rings—North, South, East, and West—are watchful spirit beings. The star represents the whole person—the flower of being. The actual structure of the star—the number of petal-points—symbolizes the work which man must do in order to achieve a harmony or resonance with a greater order. Through conscious mastery man may then pass through that structure which he has created, and break out of it—very much in the manner of the Zen master breaking the bottle to release its contents. Man may work so diligently and perserveringly that at one point—Phat!—a small piece of the vision of the universe opens up—and he is given a glimpse into eternity.

That eternity is represented by the deep sea-blue lying between the petal-points of the star-flower. The blue of the eternal heavens surrounding the star is the same blue which is in the center of the Mandala. It is part of the limitless source. As man becomes more diffuse—as the centripetal movement increases, his roles grow more numerous. However, the potential for unification exists—and the blue heaven is a reminder.

Placed within the North, South, East, and West petal-points are cardinal totemic medallions. The significance which is attached to them depends upon whomever views them, for they serve as a mirror, reflecting the primary reference points of culture and personality. These four points, along with the fifth—the center—afford man the point of transformation, so that he may leap through another ring of fire-light. Revealed within the northeast, northwest, southeast, and southwest points are intimations of farther universes, reminding man of his originless round.

About the star-flower is a circle of suns. If the star is man's total being, the band of suns represents the simple fact that there are a numberless amount of men, flowers, beings, and suns in the universe. And for the light to circulate it must move through all things, near and far, visible and invisible. Around this band of suns is a larger barrier of fire-light, from which two side profiles emanate. The multi-faceted noses, outer channels of the breath of the circulation of the light, are the most prominent feature. The lips of these beings form the two quarter-circle rims along the bottom left and right-hand corners of the painting.

Superimposed on these side profiles is a frontal view of a face; the eyes encircle the northwest and northeast points of the star-flower. The upper part of the mouth touches the southern petal-point of the star-flower. The crown or antennae reach from the northern point of the circle of suns to the upper left and right-hand corner quarter-circles. Further description of these spirit beings is difficult, since discovering and rediscovering them is a rather subtle and personal process. Each man sees uniquely. But the basic template is there.

The outer yellow and blue violet fire-bands—complementary colors which produce a flashing effect—serve to draw the meditator in or out of the Mandala, intimating that the meditator does not stop simply with the painting, which is merely an extension or crystallization of life. Finally, at the four corners are apparitions of four primal guardians. These spirit beings are protectors, emphasizing the initiatory aspect of this Mandala. The pulsing of the yellow and

blue fire-bands, the fire-light rings, the colors and forms of the entire painting relate to the union of breath and heart, allowing "the circulation of light" to flow unimpeded.

Man is at once the most recent and highly organized species of the planet. He is the creature who, by virtue of his "newness," is the repository of all of that which precedes him down to the originless origin of all things. Because of these characteristics he is also the creature with the most to organize and integrate. His work is tremendous. Man has scarcely begun. As George Ohsawa has pointed out, if one galactic revolution of the solar system takes two hundred million years, and this is comparable to one galactic year, on this scale, man is only nine days old.

The conflict which surrounds and pervades man is little more than birth pangs—kickings and screams. Even though man is the most complexly organized creature, the "work" which he is to achieve through himself is essentially no different in process, structure, or principle, than that of the flower. Man is raw and unformed; the totality of his species has yet to form itself into the living Mandala of planetary creation. Man has found his strength—and more than proudly displayed it—now he must learn to control it. To change and yet to take on definite forms, to be of matter and yet penetrate beyond it; to become a resonator and an antenna, "grounding" the higher energies necessary for the next evolutionary stage in which man transforms the earth—this is the birth process of the present.

We mutually worked upon our vision of this "birth process": *In order for there to be a new birth, the Mage must move across the Earth* (see Plate 14). The period during which we collaborated upon this painting corresponded to the length of Miriam's pregnancy. The time of the pregnancy seemed most appropriate to join forces on one effort that would consolidate our energies for the coming ritual of birth. The growth of the painting through the months was like a psychic reflection of the process occurring in the womb. Wondrous and new, the being expanding Miriam's belly rose up in a totemic explosion of serpentine light.

As a vision of the magic of coming-into-being, this painting evokes the art of the neolithic cave sanctuaries—the mystery of life is celebrated in an intermingling of transiency and transcendence, highlighted by the ethereal appearance of the hand and footprints of the parents-to-be. Just as it had been necessary to come together in order for our child to come into being, we found that to become more than merely the sum of two individuals we had to immerse ourselves once again in a group Mandala. Through the mandalic process we were submitting to a greater source—the common root from which all individual beings spring.

Radiant Man and Radiant Woman

Self-renewed and recreated as a family, we found the strength to return to our individual centers only to see there reflections of each other. To say that I am only woman—*yin*—or I am only man—*yang*—is an illusion. All phenomena.in the universe are an admixture of these two aspects of the unifying principle and each thing is ultimately a projection of this unity. *Radiant Woman*—agent of the *yin* principle—was executed by the man, and *Radiant Man*, by the woman (see Plate 15). For each of us it was an exercise in projecting the qualities supposedly opposite to our respective genders. We worked together on these paintings for almost a year, and through this process gained a deeper appreciation of the universal *yin-yang* nature.

To understand "woman," the characteristic most descriptive of *yin* must be meditated upon—receptive devotion—but only as it is an attribute of the unifying principle. Likewise with *yang,* whose chief characteristic is an all-pervading initiatory power. These qualities are necessary complements of each other. A man denying himself the quality of receptive devotion is an arrogant tyrant; a woman denying herself the energy of the initiatory power is a barren vessel. The unifying power, Tao—the universal law—is both. Where can the power initiated by the primal source go if not into the vessel of receptive devotion, and what can this receptive element receive if not the divine energy of the initiatory power?

In the paintings of *Radiant Man* and *Woman* devotion is signified by the hands raised above the head. Alpha and Omega are in the hands of the man, in the woman, the nuclear signs of creation itself. The Alpha and Omega hands of devotion beneath *Radiant Woman* display the reverence which man must give to that element which bears and nourishes him. All of creation praises the creator in as many ways as there are forms and ways of being. Each creature in its very essence is an act of praise, and the natural outlet of praise is devotion. Within every man there is a woman receiving. Within every woman there is a man who gives boundlessly. The conscious realization of the dynamic co-existence of the two elements within an individual gives rise to an aura of radiant beauty and joy.

In *Radiant Woman* the aura literally bursts forth; in *Man* it is more subdued. *Woman,* the receptive, carried on a bed of outstretched serpent forms, opens her bounties to the light. *Man,* the initiator, stands firm in the night. The inner ring of the *Woman's* aura is a cycle of moons in a band of fire—*Man* emits the mirrored aura in which all things are clearly distinguished. At the feet of *Woman* is the pool of the Tao, from which rises and into which descends a lotus ladder. In the limbs of these radiant beings are the intertwined forms of organic extension, mingled with script and hieroglyphs of astral sight—it is not the eye alone that sees, it is not the mind alone that perceives, everywhere is written the language of creation and it takes only the eye of devotion to read it.

Filling the body proper of the *Radiant Man* and *Woman* are energy centers, the Chakras. Psychophysical integration occurs through the interdependent functioning of these centers. The lowest energy center is the root Chakra. In *Radiant Man* this is a twelvefold seed containing the symbols of the cycle of the sequence of change—both from astrology and the *I Ching.* From the root center of *Woman* an actual organism emanates—what is potential in *Man,* becomes actual through *Woman.*

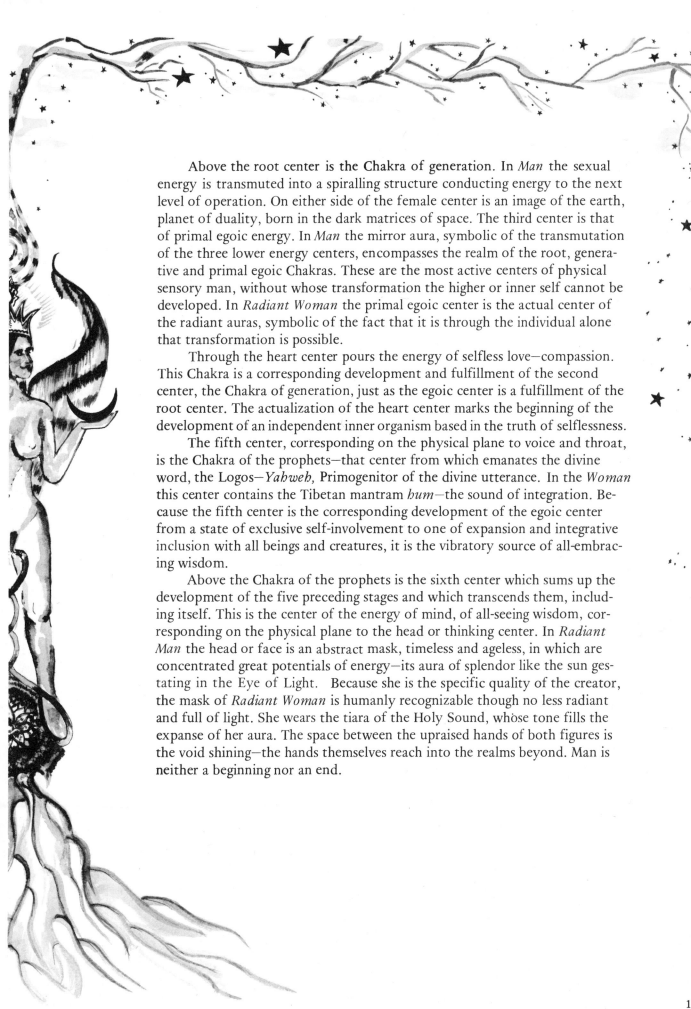

Above the root center is the Chakra of generation. In *Man* the sexual energy is transmuted into a spiralling structure conducting energy to the next level of operation. On either side of the female center is an image of the earth, planet of duality, born in the dark matrices of space. The third center is that of primal egoic energy. In *Man* the mirror aura, symbolic of the transmutation of the three lower energy centers, encompasses the realm of the root, generative and primal egoic Chakras. These are the most active centers of physical sensory man, without whose transformation the higher or inner self cannot be developed. In *Radiant Woman* the primal egoic center is the actual center of the radiant auras, symbolic of the fact that it is through the individual alone that transformation is possible.

Through the heart center pours the energy of selfless love—compassion. This Chakra is a corresponding development and fulfillment of the second center, the Chakra of generation, just as the egoic center is a fulfillment of the root center. The actualization of the heart center marks the beginning of the development of an independent inner organism based in the truth of selflessness.

The fifth center, corresponding on the physical plane to voice and throat, is the Chakra of the prophets—that center from which emanates the divine word, the Logos—*Yahweh,* Primogenitor of the divine utterance. In the *Woman* this center contains the Tibetan mantram *hum*—the sound of integration. Because the fifth center is the corresponding development of the egoic center from a state of exclusive self-involvement to one of expansion and integrative inclusion with all beings and creatures, it is the vibratory source of all-embracing wisdom.

Above the Chakra of the prophets is the sixth center which sums up the development of the five preceding stages and which transcends them, including itself. This is the center of the energy of mind, of all-seeing wisdom, corresponding on the physical plane to the head or thinking center. In *Radiant Man* the head or face is an abstract mask, timeless and ageless, in which are concentrated great potentials of energy—its aura of splendor like the sun gestating in the Eye of Light. Because she is the specific quality of the creator, the mask of *Radiant Woman* is humanly recognizable though no less radiant and full of light. She wears the tiara of the Holy Sound, whose tone fills the expanse of her aura. The space between the upraised hands of both figures is the void shining—the hands themselves reach into the realms beyond. Man is neither a beginning nor an end.

The Mandala is a path leading to the realization of the restructured individual as a self-sustaining and self-illumined whole. To project into the future is only to speak of the potential of the present. If man can mandalize himself, there will be a resulting deployment of now unused energies within his bio-organic structure. It is these energies which will be most instrumental in creating a radiant—radiating from multiple centers—planetary sphere. This is what is implied in Teilhard de Chardin's "noosphere," a glowing, pulsing aura, a phosphorescent psychic plasma, earth's last sheath expanding and opening in her mating with the reaches of cosmic space. To realize this vision, courage to change is the the chief prerequisite; to simplify and yet expand, to purify and integrate, to individuate and interrelate with all other forms and evolutionary possibilities—*this* is the destiny of man.

Because it contains the origins of beginnings, the Mandala is a means to man's evolutionary future. The visualization and creation of the Mandala receives its consecration when the individual realizes himself as all things, knowing that the Mandala has been embodied within him. Incorporation of the Mandala becomes a preparation for transformation. A deepening insight is born, transcending the ordinary and all-too-narrow boundaries of the everyday as it comes to be lived in the inevitable course of thought-systems which grow, mature, and decay like all conditioned phenomena.

Unless our attitude toward it changes, the world itself will never change. The change in attitude must be firm in its root, stable at its base, and whole in its fruit. If an attitude can be changed, then the world-structure which that attitude presupposes will also change. This is brought about by passing through the gates of fear—fear, ignorance, and desire are what lock one attitude into place and which consequently put into bondage the individual's ability to act openly and be at peace with himself.

> *The common way of appearance that is to be abandoned is not the world as it appears before our senses, but our feelings and ideas about it. . . . The conquest consists in the eradication of the common way of appearance and of the appetite for it by changing one's feelings and ideas about it when that which one has clearly imagined stands before one's mind in all its transparency. This happens when, in imagining the world and its inhabitants as a* mandala *and in feeling oneself as transfigured, both the capacity for feeling transfigured and the* mandala *are clearly present before one's mind. It is not enough to bring about a little change for a while, it must be a stable experience.*
>
> Tsong-kha-pa

In the full process of the Mandala there is a return to the point of origin. The return depends upon the transference of the mind-contents to the projected Mandala so that the mind becomes transfigured into the Mandala. Because of this mental change the process of the everyday slowly becomes mandalized. Basic bodily functions are experienced as an interrelated whole; feelings and emotional dispositions receive their colors and cardinal points; modes of perception are distinguished and take their places in the compass of being; the will and volitional tendencies become harmonized accordingly; consciousness is transformed into a discriminating tool at once beyond all condition and conception, and at the same time immersed in the perpetual flow of change. The world and its inhabitants are realized as integral facets of one Mandala.

In the Tibetan yogic rite of Non-Ego, the change of attitude is symbolized by an offering of the Mandala conceived as the yogin's own body. This body-Mandala is imagined as being constituted of every desirable worldly thing. In offering himself, the yogin recites:

This illusory body which I have held to be so precious
I dedicate in sacrifice as a heaped-up offering
without the least regard for it, to all the deities
that constitute the visual assembly:
may the very root of self be cut asunder!

The mandalic attitude is neither egocentric nor necessarily anthropomorphic. Nothing is excluded; everything finds its place and is understood as an integral aspect of a whole process. And because everything is interrelated and derives meaning only through relationship, things in themselves are seen to be void of any self-nature. This openness is the basis of all things and is at the very center of the Mandala. It is what makes the mandalic attitude a perpetually transformative vision, for it is rooted in no-thing, and can adopt itself to whatever configurations the life-flow presents.

The primeval Mandala was doubtless a circle drawn upon the ground. Stepping forth from that circle, the initiate moved through a world of magic in which he was but a tongue of the earth chanting her song to the stars. The wheel of time returns. The magic circle is drawn once again.

Notes

The Mandala of the Curve of Developing Consciousness is essentially derived from Lama Anagarika Govinda, *The Psychological Attitude of Early Buddhist Philosophy* (London: Rider, 1961), p. 91. Whereas Govinda's chart and explanation relate particularly to the process of meditation, ours deals with the general historical-evolutive nature of consciousness as it is developed both in the individual and collectively.

Our vision also has points of contact with and has been influenced by William Blake in his prophetic books, such as "Jerusalem," *Complete Writings* (London: Oxford University Press, 1966), pp. 620, 747; or Black Elk in the already mentioned *Black Elk Speaks.* The more psychological nuances of this vision have been described by Carl G. Jung, *Psyche and Symbol* (New York: Doubleday Anchor, 1958) and *Man and His Symbols* (New York: Doubleday, 1964).

Other references in a similar vein are Dane Rudhyar, *The Planetarization of Consciousness* (New York: Harper & Row, 1972), and *Directives for New Life* (Railroad Flat: Seed Books, 1971); Lecomte Du Nouy, *Human Destiny* (New York: McKay, 1947); Jolande Jacobi, *The Psychology of Carl G. Jung* (New Haven: Yale University Press, 1962); Chogyam Trungpa, *Meditation in Action* (Berkeley: Shambala Publications, 1970); Herbert V. Guenther, *Yuganaddha: The Tantric View of Life* (Varanasi, India: The Chowkamba Sanskrit Series, 1969); Ajit Mookerjee, *Tantra Asana; A Way to Self-Realization* (Basel: Ravi Kumar, 1971); Pierre Teilhard de Chardin, *The Phenomenon of Man* (New York: Harper Torchbooks, 1959); and Sri Aurobindo, *The Future Evolution of Man* (Pondicherry: Sri Aurobindo Ashram, 1963).

"The Four Armed Sun-God" is from *The Psychology of Carl G. Jung,* by Jolande Jacobi (Routledge & Kegan Paul, Ltd., London, 1942). The alchemical diagram on page 113 is from *A Christian Rosenkreutz Anthology,* compiled and edited by Paul M. Allen (Rudolf Steiner Publications, Blauvelt, New York, 1968).

To meet myself in beauty
To submit to the way of the Light
To realize the truth of the warrior:
            Life is suffering
Within each suffering center lies
            desire demand death

I grieve and mourn the loss of oneness
The vision of wholeness
Hidden behind the black greed of grasping eyes

O that suffering could be seen as it is:
            A state of contraction
            And withdrawal from the Path of Light

But only by passing through the burning flame of wisdom
Do the warriors' souls become strengthened
Then do they rejoice

Dancing to the noiseless sound of the universal
Turning one heart to all faces
Seeing one face in all hearts
Aflame with the healing power of love

Their chant is blessing
The Morning Star breaks in their song
All creatures rise in radiance at its shining
And even the grasses whisper

Light is eternal
It is the eye and wellspring of the creator

Bibliography

I. Mandala in the Tibetan Tradition

Sadhanamala Bhattacharya, *A Buddhist Tantric Text of Rituals* (Baroda: Gaekwad, 1928).

John Blofeld, *The Tantric Mysticism of Tibet* (New York: E.P. Dutton, 1970).

Edna Bryner, *Thirteen Tibetan Tankas* (Indian Hills: Falcon's Wing Press, 1957).

John Brzostoski, *Tibetan Art* (New York: The Riverside Museum, 1963).

Carin Burrows, *Tibetan-Lamaist Art* (New York: Henri Kamer Gallerie, Inc., 1970).

Schuyler Cammann, "The Suggested Origin of the Tibetan Mandala Paintings," *The Art Quarterly,* Spring, 1950.

L. Chandra and R. Vira, *A New Tibeto-Mongol Pantheon,* 17 volumes (New Delhi: International Academy of Indian Culture, 1959).

Garma C. Chang, *Teachings of Tibetan Yoga* (New Hyde Park: University Books, 1963).

W.E. Clark, *Two Lamaistic Pantheons* (New York: Paragon, 1937).

Jean Eracle, *L'art des thanka et le bouddhisme tantrique* (Geneva: Musée d'ethnographie, 1970).

W.Y. Evans-Wentz, *Tibetan Book of the Dead* (London: Oxford University Press, 1960).

_____, *The Tibetan Book of the Great Liberation* (New York: Oxford University Press, 1968).

_____, *Tibet's Great Yogi, Milarepa* (London: Oxford University Press, 1928).

_____, *Tibetan Yoga and Secret Doctrines* (New York: Oxford University Press, 1958).

A. Foucher, *Catalogue des peintures nepalaises et tibetaines de la collection B. H. Hodgson à la Bibliotheque de l'Institute Française* (Paris: 1897).

Garuda: Tibetan Buddhism in America (Barnet: 1971).

Annete K. Gordon, *The Iconography of Tibetan Buddhism* (New York: Paragon Books, 1966).

_____, *Tibetan Religious Art* (New York: Paragon Books, 1963).

Lama Anagarika Govinda, *Foundations of Tibetan Mysticism* (London: Rider, 1960).

_____, *Mandala: der heilige Kreis* (Zurich: Origo Verlag, 1960).

_____, *Way of the White Clouds* (Berkeley: Shambala Publications, 1969).

A. Gruenwedel, *Mythologie du bouddhisme en Tibet et en Mongolie* (Paris: E. Leroux, 1900).

Herbert V. Guenther, *The Life and Teaching of Naropa* (New York: Oxford University Press, 1963).

_____, *Treasures on the Tibetan Middle Way* (Berkeley: Shambala Publications, 1969).

_____, *Yuganaddha: The Tantric View of Life* (Varanasi: The Chowkamba Sanskrit Series, 1969)

Bhikku Khantipalo, *The Wheel of Birth and Death* (Kandy: The Buddhist Publication Society, 1970).

Raymonde Linoissier, *Les peintures tibetaines de la collection Loo* (Paris: 1932).

Ariane MacDonald, *Le Mandala de Manjusrimulakalpa* (Paris: Adrien-Maisonneuve, 1962).

Marie Therese Mallmann, "Etude iconographique sur Manjucri," *Publications de l'école Française d'Extreme-orient,* Volume LV (Paris, 1964).

_____, "Introduction à l'étude d'Avalokitesvara," *Annales du Musée Guimet,* Volume LVII (Paris: 1948

Odette Monod-Bruehl, *Peintures tibetaines* (Paris: Albert Guillot, 1954).

C.A. Muses, *Esoteric Teachings of the Tibetan Tantra* (Indian Hills: Falcon's Wing Press, 1961).

Newark Museum Association, *Catalogue of the Tibetan Collection and other Lamaist Articles in the Newark Museum,* 5 volumes (Newark: 1950).

Pratyapaditya Pal, *The Art of Tibet* (New York: New York Graphic Society, 1969).

_____, "The Iconography of Amogapasha Lokesvara *Oriental Art,* Volume XII, number 4, 1966, and Volume XIII, number 1, 1967.

_____, *Lamaist Art: The Aesthetics of Harmony* (Boston: Museum of Fine Arts, 1969).

G. Roerich, *Tibetan Paintings* (Paris: Guethner, 1925).

Rahula Sankrityayana, "Buddhist Paintings in Tibet," *Asia Magazine,* Volume XXXVII, number 10, October 1937, pp. 711-715.

_____, "Technic in Tibetan Painting," *Asia Magazine,* Volume XXXVII, number 11, November 1937, pp. 776-780.

_____, "Tibetan Art," *Marg,* Volume XVI, number 4, 1963.

F. Sierksma, *Tibet's Terrifying Deities* (Rutland: Charles Tuttle, 1966).

Madanjeet Singh, *Himalayan Art* (New York: Macmillan, 1965).

D.L. Snellgrove, *The Hevajra Tantra* (London: Oxford University Press, 1959).

Tarthang Tulku, *Kalachakra,* (Berkeley: Dharma Press, 1971).

_____, *The Sacred Art of Tibet* (Berkeley: Dharma Press, 1971).

Chogyam Trungpa, *Born in Tibet* (Baltimore: Penguin Books, 1971).

_____, *Meditation in Action* (Berkeley: Shambala Publications, 1970).

Guiseppe Tucci, *Land of the Snows* (London: Elek Books, 1967).

_____, *Theory and Practice of the Mandala* (London: Rider, 1960).

_____, *Tibetan Painted Scrolls* (Rome: Istituto Poligrafica Dello Stato, 1947).

S.C. Vidyabhusana, "On Certain Tibetan Painted Scrolls and Images," *Memoirs of the Asiatic Society of Bengal,* Volume 1, number 1 (Calcutta: 1905).

R. de Wojkowitz-Nebesky, *Oracles and Demons of Tibet* (The Hague: Mouton, 1956).

II. Mandala in the Indian Tantric Tradition

Art tantrique, commentaries by H. Michaux, O. Paz and S. Melikian (Paris: Le Point Cardinal, 1970).

Sri Aurobindo, *The Future Evolution of Man* (Pondicherry: Sri Aurobindo Ashram, 1963).

_____, *The Life Divine* (New York: India Library Society, 1965).

_____, *The Mind of Light* (New York: Dutton, 1971).

_____, *On Yoga: The Synthesis of Yoga* (Pondicherry: Sri Aurobindo Ashram, 1955).

Arthur Avalon (Sir John Woodroffe), *The Garland of Letters* (Madras: Ganesh, 1964).

_____, *The Great Liberation (Mahanirvana Tantra)* (Madras: Ganesh, 1963).

_____, *Hymn to Kali* (Madras: Ganesh, 1964).

_____, *Hymns to the Goddess* (Madras: Ganesh, 1964).

_____, *Introduction to Tantra Shastra* (Madras: Ganesh, 1914).

_____, *Kularnava Tantra* (Madras: Ganesh, 1965).

_____, *The Principles of Tantra* (Madras: Ganesh, 1914).

_____, *Shakti and Shakta* (Madras: Ganesh, 1965).

_____, *The World as Power* (Madras: Ganesh, 1966).

Chakra: A Journal of Tantra and Yoga, Volumes I and II (New Dehli: Kumar Gallery, 1971-72).

Ananda K. Coomaraswamy, *Dance of Shiva* (New York: Noonday Press, 1957).

_____, *Transformation of Nature in Art* (New York: Dover, 1956).

Mircea Eliade, *Yoga: Freedom and Immortality* (New York: Bollingen Books, 1958).

Equals One, "Society," (Pondicherry: 1968).

Ramana Maharshi, *Collected Works* (New York: Samuel Weiser, 1969).

Ajit Mookerjee, *Tantra Art: Its Philosophy and Physics* (Paris: Ravi Kumar and New York: Random House, 1968).

_____, *Tantra Asana: A Way to Self-Realization* (Basel: Ravi Kumar, 1971).

P. H. Pott, *Yoga and Yantra* (The Hague: Martinus Nijhoff, 1966).

Rama Prasad, *Nature's Finer Forces* (Madras: Theosophical Publishing House, 1933).

Phillip Rawson, *Erotic Art of the East* (New York: Putnam, 1968).

The Song of God: Bhagavad Gita, translated by Swami Prabhavananda and C. Isherwood (New York: Mentor Books, 1954).

The Upanishads, edited by Swami Nikhilananda (New York: Harper Torchbooks, 1963).

Vivekananda, *The Yoga and Other Works* (New York: Rama Krishna and Vivekananda Center: 1953).

Heinrich Zimmer, *Myths in Indian Art and Civilization* (Princeton: Princeton University Press, 1946).

III. Mandala in Other Oriental Traditions

Benoytosh Bhattacharya, *The Indian Buddhist Iconography* (Calcutta: K.L. Mukhopadhyay, 1968).

Titus Burckhardt, *An Introduction to Sufi Doctrine* (Lahore: Shr. Muhammed Ashraf, 1959).

_____, *Sacred Art in East and West* (London: Perennial Books, 1967).

Chang Chung Yuan, *Creativity and Taoism: A Study of Chinese Philosophy Art and Poetry* (New York: Harper Torchbooks, 1966).

Ananda K. Coomaraswamy, *The Elements of Buddhist Iconography* (Cambridge: Harvard University Press, 1935).

Abu Bakr Siraj Ed-Din, *The Book of Certainty* (New York: Samuel Weiser, 1970).

Fung Yu Lan, *A History of Chinese Philosophy* (Princeton: Princeton University Press, 1953).

Lama Anagarika Govinda, *The Psychological Attitude of Early Buddhist Philosophy* (New York: Samuel Weiser, 1970).

A.K. Griswold, *The Art of Burma, Korea, Tibet* (New York York: Graystone Press, 1968).

A Gruenwedel, *Buddhist Art in India* (Delhi: S. Gupta, 1965).

C. Humphreys, *Concentration and Meditation* (Baltimore: Penguin, 1959).

The I Ching: Or Book of Changes, translated by Richard Wilhelm, rendered into English by Cary F. Baynes, Bollingen Series XIX (copyright 1950 and 1967 by Bollingen Foundation). Princeton University Press. Short quotes from pp. 126-27, 194, 265, 266-67, 268, 318.

C.G. Jung, *The Collected Works of C. G. Jung,* 14 volumes (New York: Bollingen, 1953).

Hazrat Inayat Khan, *The Sufi Message and the Sufi Movement* (London: Barrie and Rockliff, 1964).

Lao Tzu, *Tao Teh Ching* (Baltimore: Penguin Books, 1968).

Lu K'uan Yu, *Taoist Yoga: Alchemy and Immortality* (New York: Samuel Weiser, 1970).

Mai-Mai Sze, *The Way of Chinese Painting* (New York: Vintage Books, 1959).

Charles Ponce, *The Nature of the I Ching* (New York: Award Books, 1970).

Dane Rudhyar, *Astrology of Personality* (New York: Doubleday, 1970).

Sangharakshita, *The Three Jewels* (New York: Doubleday 1970).

E.D. Saunders, *Mudra: A Study of Symbolic Gestures in Japanese Buddhist Sculpture* (New York: Pantheon, 1960).

Sawa, *Art of Esoteric Buddhism* (New York-Tokyo: John Weatherhill, 1972).

Idries Shah, *The Sufis* (New York: Doubleday, 1964).

_____, *The Way of the Sufi* (New York: E.P. Dutton, 1970).

Z.D. Sung, *The Symbols of Yi King* (New York: Paragon Books, 1969).

R. Takima, *Les Deux grands mandalas et la doctrine de l'esoterisme Shingon* (Tokyo-Paris: La Maison Franco-Japonaise, 1959).

Richard Wilhelm, *Secret of the Golden Flower* (New York: Harcourt, 1931).

IV. Mandala in the Traditions of the New World Indians

L.H. Appleton, *American Indian Design and Decoration* (New York: Dover, 1971).

H. Beyer, *Mito y simbolism del Mexico antiquo* (Mexico: Sociedad alemana mexicanista, 1965).

Edmond S. Bourdeaux, *The Soul of Ancient Mexico* (San Diego: Academy of Creative Living, 1968).

Joseph E. Brown, edited by, *The Sacred Pipe: Black Elk's Account of the Seven Rites of the Oglala Sioux* (Baltimore: Penguin Books, 1971).

Alfonso Caso, *Aztecs: People of the Sun* (Norman: University of Oklahoma Press, 1967).

Miguel Covarrubias, *Indian Art of Mexico and Central America* (New York: Alfred Knopf, 1957).

Jorge Enciso, *Design Motifs of Ancient Mexico* (New York: Dover, 1953).

Weston LaBarre, *The Peyote Cult* (New York: Schocken Books, 1969).

Reginald and Gladys Laubin, *The Indian Tipi* (New York: Ballantine, 1971).

Miguel Leon-Portilla, *Aztec Thought and Culture* (Norman: University of Oklahoma Press, 1963).

John Neihardt, *Black Elk Speaks* (Lincoln: University of Nebraska Press, 1961).

H.E.D. Pollock, *Round Structures of Aboriginal Middle America* (Washington: Carnegie Instituion, 1936).

Recinos, Goetz and Morley, *The Popul Vuh, Sacred Book of the Quiche Maya* (Norman: University of Oklahoma Press, 1959).

Gladys A. Reichard, *Navaho Religion, A Study in Symbolism* (New York: Bollingen, 1963).

Carl Ruppert, *The Caracol at Chicen-Itza* (Washington: Carnegie Institution, 1935).

Laurette Sejourné, *Burning Water: Thought and Religion in Ancient Mexico* (New York: Grove Press, 1960).

Tony Shearer, *Lord of the Dawn* (Healdsburg: Naturegraph Publishers, 1971).

_____, *The Sacred Calendar* (Denver: Western News, 1967).

D.S. Sides, *Decorative Art of the Southwestern Indians* (New York: Dover, 1961).

Jacques Soustelles, *La pensée cosmologique des anciens mexicains* (Paris: Hermann & Cie, 1940).

Clara Lee Tanner, *Southwest Indian Sandpainting* (Tucson: University of Arizona Press, 1957).

David Villaseñor, *Tapestries in Sand: The Spirit of Indian Sandpainting* (Healdsburg: Naturegraph Press, 1966).

Frank Waters, *Book of the Hopi* (New York: Viking Press, 1963).

_____, *Masked Gods* (New York: Ballantine Books, 1970).

Mary C. Wheelwright, *Beautyway: A Navaho Ceremonial* (New York: Pantheon Books, 1957).

W. Willoya and V. Brown, *Warriors of the Rainbow* (Healdsburg: Naturegraph Press, 1962).

Leland C. Wyman, *Navajo Indian Painting: Symbolism, Artistry and Psychology* (Boston: Museum of Fine Arts, 1959).

_____, *The Sacred Mountains of the Navajo in Four Paintings by Harrison Begay* (Flagstaff: Museum of Northern Arizona, 1967).

_____, *Sandpaintings of the Kayenta Navajo* (Albuquerque: University of New Mexico Publications in Anthropology, number 7, 1952).

V. Mandala in the Sacred Art of the West

Marcel Aubert, *The Art of the High Gothic Era,* (New York: Greystone Press, 1966).

_____, *French Cathedral Windows of the Twelfth and Thirteenth Centuries* (New York: Oxford University Press, 1947).

Ellen Judith Beer, *Die Rose der Kathedral von Lausanne und der Kosmologische Bilderkreis des Mittalters* (Bern: Benteli Verlag, 1952).

Ananda K. Coomaraswamy, *Christian and Oriental Philosophy of Art* (New York: Dover Books, 1956).

Henri Focillon, *The Art of the West in the Middle Ages* (New York: Phaedon Publishers, 1963).

Fulcanelli, *Le mystère des cathedrals et l'interpretation esoterique des symboles hermetiques du grand oeuvre*

(Paris: Eugène Canseliet, 1964).

René Gilles, *Le symbolisme dans l'art religieux.* (Paris: La Colombe, 1961).

Jean Gimpel, *The Cathedral Builders* (New York: Grove Press, 1961).

Louis Grodecki, *The Stained Glass of French Churches* (London: L. Drummond, 1948).

George Lesser, *Gothic Cathedrals and Sacred Geometry*, 3 Volumes (London: A. Tiranti, 1957-64).

Emile Mâle, *The Gothic Image: Religious Art in France in the Thirteenth Century* (New York: Harper, 1958).

Erwin Panofsky, "Abbot Suger of St. Denis," *Meaning in the Visual Arts* (New York: Doubleday, 1957).

_____, *Gothic Architecture and Scholasticism* (New York: Meridian Books, 1958).

Gerardus van der Leeuw, *Sacred and Profane Beauty: The Holy in Art* (New York: Holt Rinehart, Winston, 1963).

Otto von Simson, *The Gothic Cathedral* (New York: Pantheon Books, 1962).

Elisabeth von Witzleben, *French Stained Glass* (London: Thames and Hudson, 1968).

VI. Mandala Related to Science: Esoteric and Modern

Paul M. Allen, *A Christian Rosenkreutz Anthology* (Blauvelt: Rudolf Steiner Publications, 1968).

José Argüelles, *Charles Henry and the Formation of a Psychophysical Aesthetic* (Chicago: University of Chicago Press, 1972).

Edwin Babbit, *Principles of Light and Color* (New Hyde Park: University Books, 1967).

Faber Birren, *Color Psychology and Color Therapy* (New Hyde Park: University Books, 1961).

_____, *Color: A Survey in Words and Pictures* (New Hyde Park: University Books, 1963).

Titus Burckhardt, *Alchemy* (Baltimore: Penguin, 1971).

Robert S. DeRopp, *The Master Game* (New York: Dell Publishing Co., 1968).

Mircea Eliade, *The Forge and the Crucible: The Origins and Structure of Alchemy* (New York: Harper Torchbooks, 1971).

R.L. Gregory, *Eye and Brain: The Psychology of Seeing* (New York: McGraw-Hill, 1966).

Manley P. Hall, *The Secret Teachings of All Ages* (Los Angeles: The Philosophical Research Society, Inc., 1969).

Preston Harold and Winifred Babcock, *The Single Reality* (New York: Dodd Mead and Co., 1971).

Carl G. Jung, *The Collected Works of C.G. Jung,* 14 volumes (New York: Bollingen, 1953).

_____, *Man and His Symbols* (New York: Doubleday, 1964).

_____, *Psyche and Symbol* (New York: Doubleday Anchor, 1958).

C.W. Leadbeater, *The Chakras* (Madras: The Theosophical Publishing House, 1927).

_____, *Thought Forms* (Wheaton: The Theosophical Publishing House, 1967).

Timothy Leary, *High Priest* (New York: New American Library, 1968).

Michael Maier, *Atalanta Fugiens,* translated and edited by H.M.E. De Jong (Leiden: E.J. Brill, 1969).

Ralph Metzner, *Maps of Consciousness* (New York: MacMillan, 1971).

Ralph Metzner and Timothy Leary, "On Programming Psychedelic Experiences," *Psychedelic Review,* number 9, 1967, pp. 4-19.

Guy Murchie, *Music of the Spheres,* 2 Volumes (New York: Dover, 1967).

Lecomte Du Nouy, *Human Destiny* (New York: McKay, 1947).

S.G.J. Ousley, *Colour Meditations* (London: L.N. Fowler Co., Ltd, 1949).

P.D. Ouspensky, *In Search of the Miraculous* (New York: Harcourt, Brace, 1949).

_____, *Tertium Organum: A Key to the Enigmas of the World* (New York: Vintage Books, 1970).

Oliver Reiser, *Cosmic Humanism* (Cambridge: Schenkman Publishing Co, 1966).

Dane Rudhyar, *Astrology of Personality* (New York: Doubleday, 1970).

_____, *Directives for New Life* (Railroad Flat: Seed Books, 1971).

_____, *Humanistic Astrology Series*, 6 Volumes (Lakemont: C.S.A. Press, 1969).

_____, *The Planetarization of Consciousness* (New York: Harper and Row, 1972).

Secret Symbols of the Rosicrucians, (Los Angeles, Philosophical Research Society, 1967).

Charles T. Tart, *Altered States of Consciousness* (New York: John Wiley and Sons, 1969).

Pierre Teilhard De Chardin, *The Phenomenon of Man* (New York: Harper Torchbooks, 1959).

Allan Watts, *Joyous Cosmology* (New York: Vintage, 1962).

VII Miscellaneous Texts Related to the Mandala as a Form in Art and Nature

Steve Baer, *Dome Cookbook* (Corrales: 1969).

William Blake, *Complete Writings* (London: Oxford University Press, 1966).

Domebook One and *Domebook Two* (Los Gatos: Pacific Domes/Random House, 1970).

Mircea Eliade, *The Two and the One* (New York: Harper Torchbooks, 1969).

_____, *Rites and Symbols of Initiation: The Mysteries of Birth and Rebirth* (New York: Harper Torchbooks, 1965).

A.P. Elkin, *The Australian Aborigine* (New York: Doubleday, 1964).

Douglas Fraser, *Village Planning in the Primitive World* (New York: Braziller, 1968).

R. Buckminster Fuller, *World Design Decade Documents 1965-1975* (Carbondale: World Resources Inventory Office, 1965).

Gerald Hawkins, *Stonehenge Decoded* (New York: Doubleday, 1965).

Hans Jenny, *Kymatics* (Basel: Basilius Press, 1967).

W. Kandinsky, *Concerning the Spiritual in Art* (New York: Wittenborn, 1948).

Gyorgy Kepes, edited by, *Structure in Art and Science* (New York: Braziller, 1965).

Lama Foundation, *Be Here Now* (New York: Crown Press, 1971).

Ernest Lehner, *Symbols, Signs and Signets* (New York: Dover, 1969).

M.E.L. Masters and Jean Huston, *Psychedelic Art* (New York: Grove Press, 1968).

W.M. Matthews, *Mazes and Labyrinths: Their History and Development* (New York: Dover, 1970).

Leinani Melville, *Children of the Rainbow: The Religion, Legends, and Gods of Pre-Christian Hawaii* (Wheaton: The Theosophical Publishing Co., 1969).

Charles Mountford, *Art, Myth and Symbolism of Arnhem Land* (Melbourne: Melbourne University Press, 1956).

Bruno Munari, *The Circle* (New York: George Wittenborn, 1968).

Frank Popper, *Origins and Development of Kinetic Art* (London: Studio Vista, 1968).

Ad Reinhardt, "A Portend of the Artist as a Yhung Mandala," *Art News,* 1956.

M.C. Richards, *Centering* (Middletown: Weslyan University Press, 1964).

Theodor Schwenk, *Sensitive Chaos: The Creation of Flowering Forms in Water and Air* (London: Rudolph Steiner Press, 1968).

Richard Shannon, *The Book of Peace* (New York: Doubleday, 1971).

T.C. Stewart, *The City as an Image of Man* (London: Latimer Press, 1970).

D.W. Thompson, *On Growth and Form* (New York: Cambridge University Press, 1961).

L.L. White, *Aspects of Form* (Bloomington: Indiana University Press, 1951).

Gene Youngblood, *Expanded Cinema* (New York: E.P. Dutton Co., 1971).

We are grateful to Dane Rudhyar, Khiegh Dhiegh and Baba Hari Dass for their counsel and wisdom; to Edith Tarcov and Maggie Puckett for their persevering understanding and efforts in reading and correcting the manuscript; and to the artists—Roberto Mattiello, Ra Morris, Jeanette Stobie, Henry Sultan and Dion Wright for their cooperation and belief in the inspiration guiding this effort. Thanks to the photographers—Rod Dungan, Woody Hirzel, Yael Joel and Myron E. Collingwood, who patiently gave of their time and skill; to Lee Nelson, who set the type, and also to Robert Steiner, who did the calligraphy.

The Mandala is infinite and in any work of this nature not all points can possibly be touched upon, much less explored. We gladly welcome the reader's comments, suggestions and insights as a growing part of that Mandala which is the work of the Whole of Man.

José and Miriam Argüelles
c/o Shambala Publications, Inc.
1409 Fifth Street
Berkeley, California 94710

JOSÉ ARGÜELLES was born in Rochester, Minnesota in 1939, and spent his early childhood in Mexico. He received a Ph.D. in the History of Art from the University of Chicago in 1969. He has taught at Princeton University, University of California, Davis, and is currently Coordinator of the Man and Arts Program at the new experimental Evergreen State College in Olympia, Washington. He has written *Charles Henry and the Formation of a Psychophysical Aesthetic* (University of Chicago Press, 1972), articles on art and culture, and poetry. He is also a painter, and for the last five years has worked with his wife in exploring the potential of the Mandala.

MIRIAM ARGÜELLES was born in Chicago in 1943. She received an M.A. in the History of Art from the University of Michigan in 1966. She has had experience in film and communications media. Her work as an illustrator includes collaboration with poet Stephen Levine on *Lovebeast* (Unity Press, 1972). Her background as a painter has involved her in various exhibits, a mural project, and workshops which she has conducted with her husband.